WIRING JUSTICE

FROM THE ARCHIVES OF JOSEPH J. BALLIRO, ESQUIRE

Case: Domainio; 89-08756

by

Joseph J. Balliro, Jr.

Table of Contents

iii

iv

PROLOGUE
Death

There could be no doubt Tommy was terminal. He would have died from guilt or fear eventually, had he not submitted to death by ego, stupidity, women, and greed. Of all these distasteful faults, however, he excelled in stupidity. Had he not become so accomplished in ignorance, he would have realized he was about to be reaped. He might have figured he could run. Fear would've gotten those lizard legs going real fast. But, he probably couldn't figure that would help. He was just too stupid. Tommy Francone was just an authentic stupid son-of-a-bitch. He raced towards dust, doing and saying things that could only be paid back with agony. He had earned a death, and a very nasty one at that. After all, when you stole from Tony, there were certain guarantees. Tommy's actions were a slow persistent self-mutilation. Eventually he would die from his wounds.

It bears reporting that Tommy was driven in his excesses by the same fear that would have made those lizard legs go. Over the years of fighting his way up ladder of success, he was continuously scarred by the emotional flagellations of a guilty coward. Afraid, he tortured himself with the fear of discovery. As a balance of some sort, he tortured others in return.

Accorded a respect far greater than his own small stature, Tommy could, with a snap of his fingers, command the appearance of very large associates to commit his atrocities. They assured his position in the community remained intact. He need not concern himself with ever proving himself physically, he was too cowardly to go one-on-one with anyone, except for business' sake he occasionally slapped someone around while the big boys were behind him. He enjoyed that. Especially in public at the Cafe Pompeii on Hanover Street. Business, after all, was business, and business was tough. Tommy walked, spoke, dressed, and laughed tough. Being cocky was a way of life. If you did it right, you lived the life, if you did it wrong, the coward showed. When the coward showed you died.

Tommy's coward was showing.

The drugs sped up his return to consciousness. He got stronger as he became more aware, but he couldn't move. His jaw muscles began to work his upper and lower teeth, his breathing became short and quick, and he felt a false increase of physical prowess as he struggled with the ropes around his thighs, ankles, and arms.

They had overdosed him with speed. The sensations were coming too fast. One moment he had been unconscious, in the next moment, he was wide-eyed and petrified.

Normally Tommy enjoyed the jump he would get from the drug. It kept him sharp and hard when it was called for and made him feel strong and invincible. Sometimes he would kick start one of Tony's broads so she would fuck him and any other john all night. He had liked the feeling of power and the envy of his friends and associates.

Tied to the underside of the pier in East Boston, shot up with enough speed to turn over a cold tractor-trailer, gagged and definitely headed for death, all he could do was plead with his eyes, show the coward, and hope it would kick start some compassion in his captors.

"I'll do it for you Georgie if ya don't wanna get wet and smell like East Boston pussy all night," Tommy heard from above.

"Nah, Tony wants a special. I gotta do it myself. Get the fuck out of my way," another voice answered gruffly.

Tommy recognized the second voice as Georgie. He remembered getting into the car. He admitted stupidity to himself - finally - with the unforgiving hindsight of regret. "If only I hadn't got into that car," he thought blithering to himself. "I knew something was wrong. I'd seen that look on Georgie's face before; but I got in anyway. Everyone was looking and I didn't want to run." Little spittles of hope for salvation began to fade away as Tommy recalled his bravery. "I couldn't let people think I was afraid." He walked tough over to the car, a little challenge in his stride – "I ain't no chicken," he thought then. He pulled his expensive Gravianno suit closed and sat just as bravely into the back seat. Georgie climbed in.

They must of cold cocked him, drove him to Eastie, tied him to the pier and shot him up with speed.

He could see Georgie's legs as he climbed down the ladder set in the bottom muck of the harbor. The ladder sunk further with Georgie's weight. When Georgie was at eye level he stopped, reached into his belt, pulled free a hand hatchet, looked into Tommy's eyes and smiled. Tommy wrestled in greater panic.

"You dumb fuck, you had a good thing going but ya had to get greedy and steal from Tony," Georgie hissed. "You know what?

4

'Cause you're such a stupid fuck I get to move up the corporate ladder. Get it? Ladder," Georgie said gripping the ladder and shaking it slightly. "First though, I get to fire you, you dumb ass. Something I will enjoy greatly. I'd tell you that you'll make great fish food but we both know they'll only get the scraps."

Georgie climbed down and stood in the harbor bottom. His chest was at knee height to Tommy. Before administering justice Georgie commented, "I love my work." Tentacles of absolute horror tightened Tommy's binds as he realized the inevitability and finality of the next moments.

Georgie raised the hatchet above his head and struck down on Tommy's leg.

Even though muffled, Tommy's screams were audible. His body jerked in panicked hysteria.

"Damn it to hell," Georgie exclaimed, "fucking blood on my clothes and Eastie piss puke on my shoes. Tommy you're a real asshole. If ya had kept still I wouldn't a' had to get blood on me."

Tommy screamed.

Georgie hit the other knee a good shot capping it neatly. Tears bucketed from Tommy in shudders of muffled cries. He jerked a few more times before he slumped into semi consciousness. "That's all I gotta do Tommy," Georgie explained standing on the ladder at eye height once again, "I gotta go up the ladder of success. Nice knowing you, you dumb fuck. Never learn, never fuckin' learn." Georgie shook his head, climbed onto the pier and drove away.

Tommy lasted some hours before he drown. The water was cold and soothed him for a short time until the tide rose to knee level, the salt adding fire to ice until that too numbed all feelings of pain.

In his drugged and shocked state he did not recognize that he was dinner. As the tide reached chest level he could see the cat sized bodies of the harbor rats splashing about. Attracted by the blood and excited to frenzy they tugged at his wounds. What Tommy had thought was the pressure and pull of the ocean he now realized were the rodents as they tore at his flesh. This drew him back into greater consciousness and he cried in shock. When the ocean reached his throat the rodents pushed out of the black waters grasping his lips with their small, sharp teeth. Turning his face side to side to avoid their attacks they eventually tore away at his gag. A long wail scattered them temporarily.

Tommy cried and howled until his throat seized from the salt, the cold, and the wet. He went unheard. No one but the rats came.

As death seized its moment, Tommy, lacking the strength to perpetuate his false courage, abandoned his arrogance and became the fear-child he had sheltered. It was far too late for honesty. With a face and body shredded, Tommy's weeping was unintelligible and unheard. Volume stifled by the clean slice of a blade.

Tommy died - gratefully - in the blessed and glorious tranquility of asphyxiation.

Chapter 1
A Beginning

His sisters' unleashed clamor was a constant source of early morning irritation always loud and persistent by sheer number. They knew he had the front room and they knew there was no way he could sleep with them tramping through. His mother's daily collusion in the conspiracy to wake him the least gently was especially disheartening. Hearing her voice, he surrendered to the inevitable conclusion that he would not be able to steal another moment's rest. As he came further awake, his resistance to consciousness faded. Joey knew that no matter how rude an awakening it would be warm and comfortable in his Chelsea tenement home.

The smell and heartthrob of his mother's percolator was welcoming. His ears siphoned out the loveliest of all symphonies from the combined cacophony of his sisters' anarchy. His eyes scanned a limited and familiar home and he felt the freshness of a new day like only a boy of fifteen can - a feeling men dream of in a moment of weakened adult spirit when not reflecting on the job, the bills, the taxes.

"Joey, get up, let's go!" Joanna prodded.

"Puuhhh......," he rattled, rolling off the couch onto the floor and into a fetal heap. "I'm up, I'm up!!"

- "Joey, get off the floor," he heard his mother order. "Pick up your bed sheets and get moving. Everybody's up and your always last!"

"That's because everybody always walks around my bedroom like it's a living room - wait a minute, it is a living room!" he said standing in his pajamas posing as Groucho Marks. "Hey, that was a joke, living room - bedroom, get it? What's everybody dead from the neck down this early? Or is that from the neck up?" he persisted confident in the Marks' legacy. His humor fell on uncaring ears.

"Joey, I want you to pick up the couch, put the sheets, folded, in the bedroom and get ready for school - or you will regret it young man," Anna threatened.

"I'm goin', I'm movin'," Joey doled out.

At 5:30 in the morning Joey's Chelsea home was a metropolis, its hurried activity a combination of his five sisters primping and prepping for the day, his father sitting at the kitchen table, pulled away from the wall to accommodate the five girls and Joey, reading and, as usual, drinking coffee, ignoring the commotion and every so often adding to the calamity by turning and reaching for the stove to refill his coffee which in turn triggered a sharp retort from Ann whose small frame worked the kitchen like a sergeant in the Marine Corps.

"Jim, just sit there and I'll get your coffee," Ann pleaded for the millionth time. "It's bad enough with the kids running around; I don't need you getting in the way." Commanding over her shoulder as she stirred the Quaker Oats, Ann called, "Everybody sit down for breakfast."

Once everyone was seated, Jim asked, "How are your studies goin' Joey?"

"Good Pa. We're doin' history. I think the teach' is gonna get into immigration and naturalization next."

"Well, listen to her. You'll learn how we got here."

"Pa, why don't you just tell me, then I can tell her?"

"Don't be a wise guy. Besides I don't remember much. I was a lot younger than you."

"Well, I could ask Grandpa, he'd remember."

"You can ask Grandpa anything you want but I want you to learn it the way they teach it to you. You need good grades."

"I will but I'd like to know how it really happened."

"The way they teach you is the way it really happened, not how Grandpa remembers it," Jim said.

"Pa, that doesn't make sense. The guy that wrote the book probably wasn't even alive then."

"Joey just do what they tell you," Jim said.

"There's Tony, Loraine. Let him in please?" Joey knew the knock on the kitchen door to be his friend Tony Domainio.

"Hi, Tony," Loraine said as she opened the door.

"Good morning family Balliro," cheered Tony.

"You hungry Tony?" Ann asked. "Sit down and have some breakfast."

"No thanks Mrs. Balliro, we gotta go - come on Joey."

"Joey sit there and finish your breakfast," Ann ordered.

"Ma, I'm done, look," Joey tilted up his bowl for inspection.

"Well, eat your toast," Ann conceded.

"Ma, I can't eat it. I've got nothing to dunk it in," emphasizing again his empty bowl of oatmeal.

"Just take it with you, it's got butter on it."

"Okay Ma," Joey agreed. "Let's go Tony."

Outside the tenement, the street was filled with kids heading for Chelsea High School. It was a magnificent spring day, the fever had already set into Tony and he had little intention of going to school.

"Joey, let's skip school," he teased.

"Tony, I could make millions betting on what days you want to take off. What are you gonna do all day, collection?"

"You got it," Tony said. "I got a lot of money out and I want some of these dirtballs to pay up."

"Great, Tony. You're gonna play hooky all day and hang around the playground collecting. That's real smart."

"Look, you're goin' right?" Tony asked fully expecting Joey to go to school as he always did.

"Yeah."

"I thought so, Ya always do. I tell you what, you tell Billy, Pauly boy, Guy Cappolino, and JP to meet me under the ramp across from the school. Tell them a half an hour apart from 11:00 on and I'll give you a cut of my vig."

"Great. How much is it gonna cost me to get a cut?" Joey smirked.

"Come on Joey, I said I'd give it to you," Tony said with some hint of sincerity.

"Yah, right Tony. I tell ya what, if I see them I'll tell them, but I'm not gonna go looking' for them. You can run a tab on what you owe me."

"Alright, that way you can earn interest."

"Interest!" Joey huffed. "Tony the only interest you have is in getting interest not givin' it out."

"You know Joey, best buddy; sometimes you can really hurt a guy. Shit, there that asshole Billy," Tony said spotting a client. Tony raised his voice teasingly. "Billy, Oh, Billy, you piece of shit, get your ass over here!"

Billy turned at the sound of his name, spied Tony and took off like a bullet.

"I'm gonna kill that motherfucker," Tony said to Joey without turning away from the running Billy. "He owes me fifty for two weeks and still owes me the original fifty. I'm gonna kick his ass, watch this."

Tony took off at a fast clip. Intersecting Billy with a flying tackle Tony drove him into a stack of crushed fruit crates. Tony grabbed Billy by the collar with his knee on his groin and screamed, "Where's My Fuckin' Money Asshole? I Want My Fuckin' Money Now!"

"I don't got it Tony," Billy whimpered. "I need more time."

"Time! Time! You Stupid Piece Of Shit, I Told You To Be On Time. Now You Want Me To Give You Time! You've Already Got My Fuckin' Money And Now You Want My Time! You're Out Of Time And Now You're Gonna Give Me Your Fuckin' Balls If You Don't Got My Money! And Your Gonna Give Me Your Balls Every Fuckin' Day Until You Give...Me...My...Fuckin'...Money!",Tony screamed.

Appearing to have expended his anger, Tony's face relaxed. Billy, glancing sideways through hands that sought to protect his face, saw that Tony looked calmer and indeed, had let off some of pressure on his groin. As Billy moved to shift Tony's knee, he, instead, found himself suddenly writhing in an uncontrolled panic as Tony put his weight behind his knee crushing Billy's testicles against the sidewalk. Billy screamed in pain trying to squirm deeper into the concrete beneath him. Having lowered his hands, Tony responded by punching Billy in the nose twice with an open palm smashing bone and causing blood to gush in a burst. Billy was crying and moving wildly making it impossible for Tony to maintain his balance. Tony fell to the side. Billy curled to the opposite side, eyes wide and frozen, with one hand over his testicles and one hand covering his nose and mouth. Tony became even more incensed as he looked up from the ground into the eyes of the crowd of kids that had gathered. It was demeaning and disrespectful to have been cast aside.

Tony stood up furious. Looking down at the prone Billy he said, "You just don't understand - I WANT MY FUCKIN MONEY! NOW!" he screamed and with punctuation, Tony let fly two well aimed kicks into Billy's exposed kidneys. Billy's body convulsed uncontrollably.

Joey grabbed Tony, locked his arms near his sides and pulled him off Billy. "Tony, if you kill him, you'll never get your money," he reasoned. Tony fought Joey's restraint seeking to inflict more injury on the now semi-conscious Billy. In a few seconds however Tony relaxed again and Joey released him.

Tony moved to Billy, hovering over him shortly before grabbing him by the hair, turning his head toward him and spitting in his face. With quiet insistence he said, "I want my fuckin' money, all of it, tomorrow. You understand?" There was a distinct hollow sound as Tony raised Billy's head about a foot higher off the sidewalk and slammed his face down hard on the concrete. It bounced once and came to rest. Tony turned to Joey and said, "He'll get the money now or I beat him worse tomorrow."

"Tony, he'll be lucky if he's awake tomorrow," Joey said.

"That's fuckin' right. And if he is, I'll beat him again. If not, I'll beat his fuckin' brother. I'll beat his whole fuckin' family until I get my money." Looking over Joey's shoulder, Tony said, "Let's get out of here, here comes his asshole father."

As they moved away swiftly, Tony looked down at his trousers. As he started to brush away dirt from his pant legs he commented reflectively: "Miserable piece of shit got my pants dirty."

At fifteen, in his first year of high school, ambitious Tony had cornered the young shylock market in Chelsea starting with his own small bank stolen from several small house breaks in the summer of his fourteenth year. As a reward for his imaginative application of tried and true methods of finance, enforcement and collection, Tony was awarded this territory by his father who took his customary 50% of the 100% per week interest Tony collected on the money he lent.

This stream of commerce extended far beyond the schoolyards and streets of Chelsea, merely the outskirts of the immigrant community. Based on demographics of immigrant population and finance, the Domainio enterprise corporate offices were centered in the North End of Boston. The Domainio family fiscal support system injected the necessary capital into the community otherwise denied by the formal banking institutions. Over the years, a small meat store here, a bakery there, vegetable carts, newsstands, barber shops, restaurants, flowers, churches, bars, coffee houses, corner markets, and even a building for the fire department grew from the coffers of the Domainio holdings. Here the Domainio family was the future.

For the others whose dreams were borrowed and invested at Suffolk Downs or Wonderland race track, they suffered the severity of their nightmares at the hands of the Domainio clan.

However, these were only kinks in a well-oiled machine greased by the contributions of the faithful, respectfully paying the $100.00 dollars per week on the $1,000.00 borrowed or the $250.00 dollars a week on the $2,000.00 borrowed never paying back the original loan, even though they could. This was true even when the banks, recognizing the shortfalls of their decision to redline the community, began to loan money. In the long run their interest was more of a dollar figure and an argument than that of the Domainio's. The Domainio rate never changed, even with inflation, and in Gaetano they had a friend, someone who took the chance, someone who showed he cared about his people, someone who would come to their aid when the family was in trouble or needed help. Consequently, it was personally unadvisable and bad business practice to insult that friendship by paying back the original sum.

This deistic homage would last generation to generation, building a pedestal upon which the community's consciousness was perched. A consciousness composed of a self-perpetuating ignorance blind to the atrocities committed in the name of cash flow and net profit.

For now, without the constant pressure and intervention of the police and the district attorney's office, Gaetano's power and influence grew unrestrained. These were the formative years of his family. Gaetano would take the appropriate steps to ensure tranquility. Sufficient numbers of politicians, cops, bail bondsman, prosecutors, and even, in some cases, judges, owed allegiance to Gaetano to permit him the grace of an aloofness that is usually only permitted those who are trusted or feared.

Ultimately, this purposeful ignorance coupled with affluence and power was responsible for seeding the corruption that would become the bedfellow of Boston politics.

For this day, in Chelsea, Tony nurtured his modest beginnings blind to his destiny as a symbol of the source of that political corruption. Soon, the politics that fed his family's growth would nourish more the incensed righteousness of the Commonwealth and the state would begin to clean house.

Chapter 2
Present Day
Commonwealth v. Anthony Domainio

As was his custom, Joe walked around the metal detector erected outside courtroom 8B at the Suffolk County Superior Courthouse at Pemberton Square in Boston. It was unnecessary that he show the court officer his Bar Card identifying him as a lawyer. He had been trying criminal cases in the Commonwealth for over 30 years and had enjoyed a reputation that had grown from regional to national prominence bringing with it public recognition and dominance within the legal community. So much so that even if someone working in this courthouse had never met him, marketing by the media would guarantee familiarity and that familiarity would guarantee a treatment that was equal or greater than his subjective status.

His reputation, like that of any attorney, was the backbone of his practice, nurtured carefully, protected, and a continuous focus of concern. Without it, there were no clients and without clients, there was no Joe Balliro. Faithful to Joe for its care and feeding, his reputation held itself out to be indispensable, lovingly awarding him with yet another high profile murder case. Like so many in the past, the Domainio murder case would supply Joe with all the excitement of the big leagues and an almost unlimited opportunity to be what he so much enjoyed; a trial attorney.

Joe was a legal junkie.

When he entered the courtroom court officers seated around counsel's table, newspapers open, coffee cups half-full, greeted Joe and shifted aside to give him room to set down his favorite, old and battered briefcase.

With a click of the clasps, his briefcase opened and Joe removed from its cluttered confines a yellow pad with almost unintelligible writing scrawled liberally throughout each page evidencing total disrespect for the organized lines printed for the user. He set his motions, the police reports, and other papers in stacks turning over the top page so that no one could nonchalantly peruse the material as they passed by the table. After briefly reviewing his notes he turned to Brian, a court officer he remembered from many a murder trial, and asked, "Brian is Tony in yet?"

"Yea, Joe, I think he's up there now. Transportation left an hour ago and I saw Phil in detention so they must be back by now," Brian answered.

Having stood while asking Tony's whereabouts, glasses in his right hand crowded by his pen, in a posture more akin to the patient dissection of an adverse witness's response, Joe left the table with a "thanks" and walked to the side exit of the courtroom that accessed the stairway to the holding cell. Heavy cast-iron bars followed the stairwell handrail up all flights. Joe turned left at the ninth floor landing and proceeded down the long hallway to the men's section of the detention area.

"Can I help you, counselor?" he heard from behind.

Turning, Joe saw a young unfamiliar face. "Oh, yes, I'm just going to see a client," he said.

"I'll need to see your Bar Card."

"Of course, I didn't realize it was necessary, I think I've got it right here." Joe reached for his wallet with a searching expression for in all likelihood he did not have the orange thin cardboard rectangle subscribed by the Supreme Judicial Court with him.

At just that moment a veteran officer who had been seated at the detention desk of the men's section walked around the corner and saw Joe from behind as he fingered aggressively through his pocket valise - the young officer standing purposefully in front of him.

"Hi Mr. Balliro," he hailed conspicuously. Speaking to the young officer he said, "It's quite alright. That won't be necessary Carlos. This is attorney Balliro. He's trying Tony Domainio downstairs." Turning to Joe he said with a smile, "I'll vouch for you counselor. Tony's in the front cell. I put him in a room all to hisself. Help yourself."

"Sorry Mr. Balliro," Carlos said. "I didn't recognize you. I'm new here."

"No it's my fault," Joe said. "I've been around for so long I forget protocol. Too much on my mind. Thank you."

The holding cells of the men's detention area were better than most, worse than some, especially considering that Massachusetts boasted the oldest jails in the country. Semi clean and sparsely furnished, Tony's cell was defined by a bed of metal sheeting perforated with holes and a bowl for bodily functions both plaudits of simplicity in a lonely place relegated to the task of providing a secure facility for holding the accused. The fact that Tony sat in the largest of the cells alone signified the seriousness of the offense, the importance of the defendant, and the representation he was able to secure.

The veteran officer who had helped Joe in the hallway had followed him into the front room, opened the cell and escorted both men into a smaller room, with a desk, two chairs, no restraints on Tony, and a door that could be closed.

Once the door was closed Joe asked, "How're you doing Tony?" shaking his hand.

"I'm okay Joe," Tony answered. "This is shit but I can hack it. What's goin' on?"

"They've made you an offer. I got the call at home yesterday after I left you at the jail."

"Jesus. Now!" Tony exclaimed. "We're ready to go to trial for Christ's sake."

"I know. Calm down. They know they have problems with the case and they're trying to force you to plead guilty. They're trying to cut out the odds you might be acquitted."

"Tell her to go fuck herself."

"Look Tony, do you want to hear the offer or not?" Joe asked.

"Okay, what is it."

"Second degree - you would have to plea to second. Not much different when it comes to the facts. You will have to admit on the stand that you killed Tommy but you would get parole. I don't have to tell you that if you get hooked on first degree you won't."

Joe paused awaiting a response. When none was forthcoming he launched into the standard explanation. "So, procedurally it goes like this. I announce that you want to change your plea of not guilty to guilty. The judge will ask you whether you are pleading willingly, voluntarily; whether you under the influence of drugs or alcohol; how far you went in school; if you've been threatened of coerced or forced to plead guilty; if you understand you're giving up your right to a trial in front of a jury; your right to appeal; you're right to have the Commonwealth present sufficient evidence to prove beyond a reasonable doubt you killed him. . . "

"Yah, yah I know all that shit," Tony interrupted.

"Tony, just let me finish, okay?"

"Sure Joe," Tony said with a smile, "you always gotta be so efficient."

Joe continued through the standard explanation, memorized from sheer repetition.

"So all's she's doin' is dropping life without parole on first degree to life with parole on second - how sweet."

"You got it, but that means you're eligible for parole in fifteen years or 180 months as the crow flys."

"Joe, you really think they're gonna let me out in 180 months," Tony lamented. "Shit, once they get me, they're gonna keep me, you know that. They'll keep on charging me with shit while I'm in there and the only time I'll see the street is from the window of the Sheriff's van when they take me to court on the new charges they dream up. Great fuckin' deal Joe."

"Tony, I never said it's a great deal, but at least you're not facing life without parole, which is what you'll get automatically if you're found guilty on first degree."

Tony sat there shaking his head and looking at Joe.

"Hey, they'll drop the weapons charge," Joe said with a little laugh.

"Big deal," Tony said.

After a moment Joe said: "I need an answer now Tony. Tell me what you want to do."

"Joe, it's like I said, tell her to go fuck herself."

Chapter 3
Case Review

Joe left the holding cell not necessarily disappointed; he was cleared to do what he loved, try a case in front of a jury, but satisfied he had done his job advising Tony of the plea.

Picking up Sergeant Walsh's police report, Joe intuitively skimmed past the seemingly insignificant information of date, time, and place and delved into his description of the offense. Tommy Francone had been found at low tied, strapped to the one of the columns supporting the pier in East Boston. Somebody had taken a small hand hatchet to his knees shattering the kneecaps and causing sufficient blood flow to entice the large wharf rats known to inhabit that area. The toxicology report said there was 'Speed' in Tommy's blood. The Commonwealth would argue that he had been given this drug in the hope in would keep him awake long enough so he knew he was being fed on - they were probably right. Whoever had done this certainly wasn't worried about Tommy crying out for help. The pathologist report indicated his tongue was missing; "the swollen wound is the deceased mouth showing signs of a clean slice by blade". Other wounds around the mouth were not so merciful. His missing lips and chin showed signs of small teeth with tests of saliva indicating the presence of rodents. The pathologist also estimated that Tommy had been alive up until the point he drowned from high tide. There was no question that if he hadn't passed out from blatant fear, he had lived long enough to feel his body being copiously fed on by the denizens of the docks.

Based on the pathologist's report the Commonwealth would have little difficulty fulfilling both theories of first degree murder, premeditation, the circumstances surrounding this death provided the necessary plan to execute; and second, cruel and atrocious conduct. Joe had seen cruel and atrocious in his 30 years of practice. This definitely fit the picture.

Although the case was well rounded in its sex appeal, liberally salted with tabloid type sensationalism, in a clinical evaluation it was clear that the Commonwealth was going to have difficulty connecting the defendant to Tommy Francone's death. The thread from which the Commonwealth hoped to spindle Tony's hangman's noose were words memorialized in a document held in Joe's hands.

The transcripts marked 'Confidential' were verbatim reproductions of surveillance tapes made of Tony and a person yet to be disclosed by the Commonwealth but whose identity was unquestionable. From any layman's perspective these tapes were damning. From a legal perspective the conversation started out fairly innocently becoming weakly equivocal at about the 20th line:

Tony D.:   "I want you to take care of that fuck, tonight."

Unknown: "Special?"

Tony D.:   "Yeah, make it a special. I got a hard-on for this asshole. He's been skimmin' off the broads for months. He's got to have eaten about 50 grand. Use your own imagination, I trust yah. Ya always did good."

Unknown: "Thanks Tony. I try. Where do you want it left?"

Tony D.:   "Eastie. Yah, Eastie. Make a mess, but don't let it go too quick."

Unknown: "Jesus, Tony, this guy's been with ya a long time. You sure ya want a special?"

Tony D.:   "Just do the fuck what I tell

ya, will ya? I don't have time
for this shit.

Unknown: "Sure Tony, sure. I didn't mean
Nothing. I just thought you
might be mad and change
your mind later. Just checkin'.
I won't see ya until tomorrow
and you want it tonight. Just
checkin'."

Tony D.: "Everybody's a fuckin' boss.
Everybody's a fuckin' thinker.
Don't think, just fuckin' do.
No, I take it back. Just think
on the things you think on
great. Be fuckin' creative, will
ya. And do your fuckin' job."

Unknown: "You got it Tony. You'll like
it. I promise you'll like what I
do. I got ideas right now.
Trust me. You'll like what I
do."

Tony D.: "Good. Now I need to see ya
tomorrow for a talk. I think
your gettin' too dirty. I'm
gonna move you into Tommy's
slot."

Unknown: "Great, Tony. I always knew I
could handle the broads and I
won't rip ya off, Tony. Fuck

that shit. I'll do my job just like I always done. I'm no trouble."

Tony D.: "You know what your problem is? You can't shut up. Just shut your fuckin' mouth. Yes or no. That's all I want to hear unless I asked you or somethin' else. You do that, we'll get along great.You got it?"

Unknown: "Sure, Tony, sure, no problem."

Tony D.: "I love it, a quick learner. You'll do good. Now do what I tell ya."

Unknown: "Ciao, Tony."

Tony D.: "Ciao, he says. Fuckin' ciao. A fuckin' Irishman says ciao. Go do some fuckin' work will ya?"

Unknown: "I'm gone Tony."

With pen in hand Joe heavily scored that section of transcript that read: 'I won't see ya until tomorrow and you want it tonight'.

Joe noted a time discrepancy for future reference. According to the transcript Tommy was supposed to die on March 2nd. The pathologist had his death on March 3rd.

If this was the Commonwealth's complete case an acquittal would have been a walk in the park. It's hard to walk, though, when someone cut's your legs out from under you. This time, Tony's legs had been chopped off big time by the confidential informant. The Commonwealth had flipped Charlie Bottatelli. Joe knew who Charlie was. He wasn't the hitter. He wasn't even the man on the tape. Did the Commonwealth know? Probably not. They probably didn't care. As far as they were concerned, Charlie was the hatchet man and the man who would put Tony away for good.

Of course, Charlie Bottatelli was not called Charlie Bottatelli in the reports; he was simply given the tag "C.I.", [C]onfidential [I]nformant. Nevertheless, the question of 'who was the C.I.?' was the subject of substantial pre-trial posturing and at issue this morning.

Joe was attempting, once again, to convince the judge that he should order the D.A. to reveal the C.I.'s identity and location. Relying on the case of <u>Commonwealth vs. Balliro</u> where another court had said that the Commonwealth could not prevent the defense from accessing a key witness, Joe hoped to convince the judge to grant his request. According to <u>Commonwealth v. Balliro</u>, Joe was entitled to access to every witness for the prosecution.

From the corner of his eye, instinctively, Joe saw one court officer come out of the judge's chambers to the left of the bench and stand with his back to the wall. Recognizing this as the customary signal that the judge was exiting chambers to take his place behind the high desk in the center of the courtroom Joe stood out of habit, his eyes remaining all the while on Officer Walsh's report of the various Domainio meetings.

Peter, the court officer that Joe had noticed peripherally, banged the wall behind him with his hand twice and called out in a loud commanding voice, "All rise!"

Another court officer behind Joe and to the side wall launched into the pronouncement: "Here ye, Here ye, Here ye. All persons having business with the Suffolk Superior Court now sitting in the County of Suffolk, City of Boston, the Honorable Justice Timothy Wilton presiding, come forward now and you will be heard. God save this Honorable Court and the Commonwealth of Massachusetts. Please be seated."

Judge Wilton, walking with purpose during the officer's recitation of that centuries old idiom, took his bench and without further ado stated: "Good morning counselors."

"Good morning your Honor," was the dual response.

"Are there any preliminary matters that need to be addressed prior to selection of the jury?"

Joe spoke, as was proper. "Yes, your Honor, I would like to renew the defendant's motion for disclosure of the confidential informant."

"I'll hear you Mr. Balliro," the judge said.

"Your honor in an effort to be expedient I will defer to my previous arguments made earlier than this date when I presented to this Court the many and significant reasons for disclosure of this man's name to the defendant. I am sure the Court recognizes the importance of the disclosure of this person to the defendant's case."

"I do wish, however, to insert an additional but inextricable caveat that heretofore your Honor may not been aware. In the past weeks as we have come closer to trial I have become much more intimate with the discovery supplied to me by the Commonwealth. Given that greater focus and the intensity in preparation of this trial it has become even more apparent that without the expected testimony of this person the Commonwealth

34

will be unable to carry its burden. Simply put, this person is crucial to their case."

"Now I am mindful that this argument is a two edged sword. The more I emphasize this person's importance to the Commonwealth, the more they will argue it is necessary to protect his well-being. However, I submit to the Court that the Commonwealth has no grounds to support any inference that disclosure will threaten this person's safety. The defendant has no criminal record, is incarcerated, and has been so restrained since his arrest some 18 months ago. The confidential informant is, as far as I am aware, in perfect health. So that if it's the Commonwealth's position that the C.I. is somehow in danger from the defendant there exists no track record for that assertion. On the other hand, if it is their position that this person is essential to their case, it becomes even more critical that I have access to him and their arguments against non-disclosure fail miserably."

"It is the very importance of the C.I. that demands disclosure to and access by the defense. And I would submit, as I have in previous argument and memoranda, that non-disclosure amounts to the Commonwealth actively preventing access to this person in violation of the mandates of Commonwealth v.

Balliro. I respectfully request therefore that the identification and whereabouts of this witness be supplied to the defense and that I or one of my colleagues be granted access to him for the purposes of interview and preparation. Thank you."

"Miss Cheline do you have argument," Judge Wilton asked.

Carolyn Cheline stood eagerly, Assigned to this case 2 years earlier before Tony was indicted and during surveillance, she was not only intimately familiar with the file but had become somewhat expectant of Joe's style of presentation accepting that he was not whimsical nor personal in his approach but professional and personally non-combative in his strategy. Comfortable and flattered at being treated as a member of the elite, she sought to respond in kind; sophisticated and restrained, forceful and sincere, but not a traitor to the club to which she had been accepted.

"Yes, your honor, If I may," she said. "I don't think there is any question that the C.I. is crucial to the Commonwealth's case and I would point out to the Court that the Commonwealth would be able proceed and carry its burden with or without his testimony. But nevertheless, it is also beyond dispute that we are dealing here with not just a man but with all his tentacles; tentacles that reach throughout the community. It is those tentacles that cause legitimate concern about the C.I.'s safety. It is the Commonwealth's position, and it has been from the day of the arrest of the defendant, that he maintains control over his empire from his cell. That control, although strong, is not necessarily as strong as it would be if he were released. Indeed, that is why the court has seen fit not to issue bail in this matter. But even more so, there exists in this community, individuals over which the defendant has little access or immediate control and who may very well do anything they can to prevent the C.I. from testifying in an effort to either endear themselves to the defendant or to fulfill some misguided instruction."

"In addition, I would point out that any attempt upon the C.I.'s life would put the lives of the law enforcement officials guarding him, and perhaps even innocent members of the community, in great danger and could conceivably cost them their lives. It is therefore the position of the Commonwealth that it is in the best interests of justice not to disclose the information sought by the defense."

"Your Honor, if I might respond," Joe stood up characteristically seeking to rebut the Commonwealth and get in the last word knowing that more often than not he is permitted that non-traditional grace. "The Commonwealth again seeks to support its request for non-disclosure by alleging that there is some mythical beast running rampant through the streets of Boston over which the defendant has sole control. Yet they offer nothing besides pure speculation in support of this fictitious goliath. There has never been any evidence of this long reaching band of thugs. There can be no evidence introduced at trial establishing this dragon of monolithic proportions. I would submit that to refuse the disclosure of this information based upon such a tenuous basis will violate the rights of the defendant under both the United States Constitution and the Massachusetts Declaration of Rights."

"Okay counselors," Judge Wilton timely interrupted, "enough said. I am going to deny the defendant's motion. Is there anything else before we begin jury selection?"

"Your Honor, please note my objection to your ruling," Joe said.

"So noted Mr. Balliro."

"I would just ask that your Honor deal with the sequestration requests of the defendant."

At Joe's request, although expected, Judge Wilton ruffled through the stack of case papers on his bench, the clerk standing to assist him in the location of the correct motion.

By no means a frivolous motion in such a widely publicized case, a motion to sequester the jury is made by the defense in an effort to prevent further taint of the jury by the media during the trial and deliberation. Sequestration means isolation, discomfort, annoyance, and hardship, and would also heap upon the jury selection process enough unwanted baggage to fill the belly of a Boeing 747. If selected, court officers would be dispatched to collect the juror's necessities from their families; they could not leave. Bosses would be told employees had taken an unexpected vacation - paid. They would travel daily in tandem by bus from the Holiday Inn on Cambridge Street in Boston, would be awakened at 7 a.m. and would be told 'lights out' at 11 p.m. They would spend half of each Saturday hearing the evidence in this case. They would eat together and inevitably some would sleep together. They would have their phone calls, all reading material, their whole lives monitored by a constant hand of court officers. They would remain guests of the Commonwealth for 4 to 6 weeks and during that time they would be unable to speak about that which they would have most in common - this case - until after he had given them instructions on the law and they were told to start jury deliberations. The difficulty of and time expended in jury selection would be increased a thousand fold by sequestration, with almost every non retired juror seeking some way, most likely told to them by an attorney friend, of being excused at every possible opportunity.

Ultimately, even though selected, four jurors would not decide the guilt or innocence of Tony. Sixteen would be selected to sit in the jury box in the courtroom, but only fourteen would decide guilt or innocence. The deliberation cask spun by the clerk at the end of the case would decide whose time had been wasted and who had become indispensable.

Judge Wilton split his decision. "I am going to deny your motion to sequester the jury during the pendency of trial. I reserve my ruling on the sequestration of the jury during deliberations, but I would be willing to hear from either of you further when it comes time for jury instruction. Now are we prepared to proceed?"

"Please note my objection," Joe said once again preserving the record.

Judge Wilton called for a recess to give the court officers the opportunity to load up the courtroom with the two hundred or so potential jurors from which the sixteen would be chosen. The selection of a jury in a capital case in Massachusetts is a long and arduous procedure designed so in an effort to ensure that the defendant would be given every opportunity to make the appropriate objections and challenges to the seating of any individual.

Each potential juror in the jury pool is cloaked with a cellophane hue of neutrality that most probably would remain impenetrable. Their prejudices, biases, desires, and attitudes hidden from strangers, such as the attorneys who inspect them for selection.

In an effort to best familiarize an attorney with a particular jury, juror questionnaires are sent out randomly to potential jurors. Random and misfortune, however, are mysteriously jaded and eerily conscious companions.

Billy got notice.

Chapter 4
A Juror

"Mary, you're not gonna believe this. I gotta go for jury duty." Billy exclaimed.

"When?" questioned Mary.

"I gotta report to the Courthouse on the fifth."

Mary was now at his side in the kitchen looking over his shoulder at the letter and juror questionnaire. "You know you gotta do that or they put you in jail," she said.

"Shit Mary, they don't put you in jail for this. You just go there and tell them some garbage they don't want to hear and your out."

"I know that, but you gotta at least show up. I wonder what trial it'll be. It could be fun. You might learn somethin'."

"I know all I want to know. They never got the guys that killed my dad and I know they won't. What do I care about being a juror except to hang some asshole by the balls," he said with disgust.

"You're supposed to be fair Bill. Look, even at the bottom of that form it says when you sign it it's under perjury," Mary pointed out.

"Jesus, Mary, none of this shit means anything. How're they gonna catch you if you don't put somethin' down they think you should of? If you don't put it down how're they gonna know?"

"I don't know. But you're supposed to put it down."

"Look, just do me a favor and call Michael. He'll know about this. Maybe he can tell me what trial they're looking for."

"Yah, okay, he's probably at home eatin' dinner. I'll ring him up."

Bill learned from Michael how to avoid selection. He also learned that he might end up sitting on the Domainio murder trial.

Bill now gloated over his good fortune at being chosen for jury duty. "Mary," he called. "Mary. You're not gonna believe *this*!" he said with emphasis. "I might get that bastard Domainio. I might get his trial!!" He turned his attention back to Michael. "Mike, how do I get on the Domainio trial?" Michael explained he would be told it was the Domainio trial before being asked if he wanted to sit as a juror. "Great," Bill said and hung up without a goodbye. "I'll find out if it's Domainio," he thought. "If it isn't, I'll get out of whatever shit trial it is and hope that they send me to Domainio. If I get Domainio, I'll get that bastard."

Chapter 5
A Beginning Continued

"Hi, Pa, Mr. Lonnegan," Joey greeted the two men seated at the table with suspicion.

Joe's father, Jim Balliro had grown older than his age. The product of years of manual labor at the shipyard. Joe had grown, as well. Now a young man of impressive stature; known for his honesty and willingness to intercede as an arbiter of neighborhood disputes.

Not only was Joe surprised to see Mr. Lonnegan when he returned from classes but he was equally surprised to see a half eaten coffee cake and empty coffee cups in front of both men. The unwelcome had been fed.

"Where's Ma?"

"She's at the market," Jim responded. "Joey, after you take off your coat, come sit. Mr. Lonnegan and me have to talk to you."

"Sure Pa, just give me a minute," Joey said offering a little smile to Mr. Lonnegan. It was not returned.

Joey went into the bedroom/living room to the corner where a desk had been set up for the past year, deposited his books and hung up his coat in the living room closet. Returning to the kitchen and took a seat to the right of Mr. Lonnegan across from his father.

"What's up?" He asked.

"Joey, Mr. Lonnegan's boy Billy is in the hospital," Jim said.

"Sorry to hear that Mr. Lonnegan. Is he alright?"

"No he ain't alright," Mr. Lonnegan said in a nasty tone. "He's got a busted kneecap, a broken arm and a concussion. They gotta keep him there for a week."

Joey sat quietly. It was pretty clear Mr. Lonnegan was not in the greatest of moods. A big burly man, like his son Billy, Mr. Lonnegan, like all the Lonnegans, was not known for talking. They mostly spoke with their fists. That was why Joey was surprised to see him here with coffee cake, half eaten, in front of him like he had been playing tea time with a five year old.

"Joey. Mr. Lonnegan here says that Tony beat up Billy with a baseball bat. He wants to know what you know about it. I told him you don't see Tony much these days, what with you in college and him working the streets."

"That's right Mr. Lonnegan. I don't see Tony much these days. We've kind of separated since Tony quit high school and I went to college. When did it happen?"

"Last night," Lonnegan returned.

"Mr. Lonnegan, I was in school until 8:00 and then I came home. I didn't see Tony last night," Joe explained.

"Mr. Lonnegan isn't blaming you, Joey," explained Jim. Both Jim and Joey caught Mr. Lonnegan's "harrumph" in response. "He just wants to know if you know anything about it."

"Look Mr. Lonnegan, I haven't spent any time with Tony for about a year and a half. If you want my opinion Billy owed Tony some money, wouldn't pay, and Tony beat him up. I don't have to tell you that. Everybody on the street knows Billy is into Tony for some serious dough."

"Funny," Mr. Lonnegan said sarcastically. "I didn't. Maybe Tony just likes pickin' on Billy cause he's Irish. That's what I think."

"Mr. Lonnegan, you can think what you like, but if you're looking for some help from me, I can't help you."

"Hey kid, get this straight, I don't give a fuck who Tony is. My kid's in the hospital, hurt real bad, I'm outta work, and I can't pay for it. I'm gonna get that little prick and the ones that did this to Billy."

46

"Wait a minute; I thought you said Tony did it?" Joey asked.

"That little prick Tony had to have help. It would take three kids his size to put down my son," he said proudly. Stopping for just about one second he looked at Joey and said, "I wanna know where's I can find Tony and you better tell me you slick street scum ors I'll take you apart too!"

Joey had enough of Mr. Lonnegan mouthing off in his house.

"Ok, ok. Pa you want to put up with this garbage in your own house, ok, but I don't have to. I don't know who hurt your son Mr. Lonnegan. Frankly, I don't care. Billy's always been a wise guy and he probably got what he deserved. As far as finding Tony; one, I don't know where he is; two, I wouldn't tell you if I did, and; three, you should be grateful you can't find him because if you do and if you hurt him you better move out of state."

"See, I told ya," Mr. Lonnegan said to Jim. "I told ya your kid was involved."

"Mr. Lonnegan, I think it's time for you to leave," Jim had had enough as well. "I won't have you accusing Joey of doing anything wrong and I won't have you calling my son street scum. Get out."

"I shoulda' known you wops would stick together on this. I don't know why I even came over here," Mr. Lonnegan stood and was at the door. "You can tell that greasy prick Tony I'll find him and when I do he'll regret the day he was born."

"No I won't, Mr. Lonnegan," Joe responded. "I don't carry Tony's messages anymore and besides I don't want to be responsible for you landing in the hospital next to Billy."

Mr. Lonnegan grunted, closed the door, and could be heard stomping down the three flights of stairs to the street.

The threat of Mr. Lonnegan lingered in the air casting a sullen pale over dinner. Ann and the girls knew that things were different and remained strictly obedient to the rule that 'at the dinner table is for eating not talking'.

Jim was concerned about his son. He was clearly destined to become a lawyer and Jim was determined to block out any negative influences that might prevent Joey from obtaining his goal; such as the violent drama unfolding daily on the streets of Chelsea.

Joey was concerned about the Lonnegan's. They were a persistent and rough lot. He worried that they would harm his sisters, mother or father, and he worried that a confrontation between Mr. Lonnegan and Tony would start an all out war that would implicate him and ruin his chances. He had no concern for the Lonnegans. They and Tony were of the same mold.

After dinner Joey sat at his desk in the living room trying to apply himself to his studies but his mind wandered incessantly to the Lonnegans and Tony. Each imagined road ended in disaster with red the predominate hue. He grappled with the option of intervention, seeking to weigh the alternatives, trying to calculate what influence he might have and what the outcome of his participation would be. He saw himself as the mediator, controlling tempers, assuaging egos. But even at that level he saw the dangers of his involvement. Danger for his family if anger turned toward him, and dangers to his future if he became so entangled that extrication was impossible.

Determined to make the law a dominate part of his life, Joey had decided long ago that severing his ties with Tony, or at least distinguishing their way of life, was essential for his future. If a connection remained, he risked being labeled a mob lawyer with all the ramifications. That was if he graduated. The consequences could be worse. He might be prevented him from getting into graduate school. Without an education, Joey and his family would be relegated to the dusty tenements of Chelsea for another generation.

Forced from his studies by a crowded mind, Joey set aside his work and stood to leave, a decision reached through self-deceit for he had half convinced himself that he needed time to think outside the confines of the small tenement and that traveling the pathways of his youth would clear his head. He would speak to Tony only if he came upon him.

Jim saw Joey come around the corner of the living room into the kitchen and head for the apartment door. "Will you be out late?" he asked.

"Don't know Pa," Joey said with a sigh. "I just need time to think."

"Be careful Joey, watch yourself."

"I will Pa, don't worry."

Once outside the tenement Joey confronted the true reason for this respite and commanded that he should get down to business and speak to Tony, have it done with, and get back to work. He decided he would have to deal with the forced interdiction of Mr. Lonnegan in his life.

Joey walked purposely down Carver Street knowing that he could get information on Tony's whereabouts from the kids Tony used for collection and who customarily congregated at the corner. As he turned onto Washington Avenue he was initially surprised to see Tony's Cadillac at the corner, but then realized that Tony was probably giving out his nightly assignments. As he approached the car from the rear he could see that Tony had spotted him in the side view mirror of the vehicle, he could see him smile, wave away the crowd, and move to exit the car. He walked toward Joey with a smile on his face. "Joe, you a lawyer yet?" he said in good humor.

"Tony, how are ya? Good to see you."

"How goes the studies?" Tony said as he stopped in front of Joe with hand out.

"Good, but I better hurry up and graduate. Looks like you'll need an attorney faster than I'll become one."

"Don't count on it. I can't afford the fees so I don't get caught. What's up? I don't see you around so I figure this is a special visit. You got a problem?"

Joey was about to answer when a car took the corner adjacent to Tony's car and purposely veered into the passenger side with a loud crash pushing the Cadillac sideways against the opposite curb and forcing the tires off the rims with two loud 'pops'. Joey cried out a startled "Shit" as he realized that the driver of the attack car was Mr. Lonnegan who had apparently followed him from his house. The car backed up and rammed into the Cadillac again crushing the front fender and now scraping the car backward on its rims.

Tony exclaimed, "What the fuck!! Motherfucker!" as he ran closer to the scene. Mr. Lonnegan jumped out of his car, now stopped, steaming, nose into the Cadillac's front fender. He headed for Tony. With baseball bat raised over his shoulder he yelled, "OKAY YOU DIRT BALL COME AND GET SOME OF WHAT YOU GAVE MY KID!"

A couple of Tony's collectors ran around the rear of the smashed cars in an attempt to get behind Mr. Lonnegan. As they drew closer Mr. Lonnegan swung around and contacted the shoulder on the front man with the bat eliciting a howl of pain, turning back the others. When he turned again to confront Tony he was met with a smile and a gun.

Tony's anger had dissipated to a grin of satisfaction. He raised the gun and said, "bye, bye!" as he fired.

Mr. Lonnegan felt the bat rip from his raised hands sending shock waves through his arms. Recovering quickly, he refused to back off and reached for the now broken bat behind him all the while keeping his eyes on Tony.

"Who the fuck are you and why do you have a death wish?" Tony asked his weapon aimed squarely at Mr. Lonnegan's face. "Leave the fuckin' bat alone or I'll blow your head off!!" he ordered.

"Tony take it easy," Joey said. "His name is Lonnegan. He's Billy Lonnegan's father."

"You're that deadbeat's father? You're as stupid as he is". Tony walked a little closer to Mr. Lonnegan remaining beyond his reach. "You come here alone, bash up my car, and threaten me. You fuckin' Irish are so stupid it amazes me. The way I figure it you owe me a new car and I owe you a serious beating. Guess what? - it's time to pay up."

"Tony, let him go," Joey intervened. "You're just going to cause more trouble and I can't afford to get involved."

"Joey I think it's time for you to leave. What the hell you doin' here anyway. You gotta protect yourself. I'll talk to you later."

"Tony this is what I wanted to talk to you about. He must have followed me from my house. He was there earlier asking about you and his son. He threatened me and my family," Joey explained.

"What an asshole," Tony said looking at the angered Mr. Lonnegan. "Fuck the deals Lonnegan. You pay for my car - I fuck up your head. You cause any more problems - I kill you. So simple even a stupid Mick can understand."

"Nobody hurts my family. Especially no piece of shit wop," Mr. Lonnegan said.

"Joe, what am I supposed to do with this guy?" Tony asked Joey half rhetorically. "You tell me. You're the fuckin' lawyer."

"Let him go," Joey advised.

"That's it Joe? That's your advice? Let him go? I let him go, I gotta problem. I teach him a lesson, you say I gotta problem. What the hell's the difference."

"Let him go Tony," Joey repeated.

"Joe I think it's time you left. Go home and study. This guy won't bother your family no more."

"Tony you don't have to hurt him. There isn't any point. You let him go and nobody's going to think he got the better of you." Joey turned to Mr. Lonnegan: "Look, you owe him a car. You pay for the car and he lets you go and forgets about Billy's debt."

Tony laughed. "Wait a minute counselor, I don't forget debts. His kid borrowed three G's from me. He knew what he was doing when he borrowed it and when he didn't pay it back. Now I got his shit father comin' after me? I think you better go. I know how to handle this."

"Tony I'm asking a favor. I'm here and I'm involved. If you hurt him the word is going to get out that I was involved. For me and my family's sake you have to come to some kind of agreement."

Tony lowered the gun while looking at Joey. His cohorts moved in closer to Mr. Lonnegan grabbing him from behind. Charlie was sitting on the stoop of the corner store nursing a badly bruised arm, obviously waiting for revenge. Tony looked at Mr. Lonnegan.

"It's good that a father looks out for his kid. That's what family's all about, ain't it?" Tony philosophized. "So you get a break. But your kid don't. You owe me for a car and the three G's your kid borrowed. I figure that's six G's your into me for. That's six hundred a week until you give me the six G's in one whack. Now your kid will take about a month - a month a half - to recover. You got till he leaves the hospital. Ya see how good this is gonna work. I ain't gonna do nothin' to him cause I want him to recover. The sooner he's out, the sooner I get my money. You get an option for more time cause if you don't pay me when he gets out, I'll see that he goes back in again and you get extra time at six hundred a week. See, we all win. But I win more. You understand that you stupid Mick?"

"Fuck you wop," Mr. Lonnegan said. The collectors' grip tightened around his neck.

"You don't get a choice. I'll get to your kid. You know I will." Tony raised the gun again pointing at Mr. Lonnegan's knee. "Let him go."

Charlie called out, "Tony you ain't gonna let this fuck go. I think he broke my arm."

With a slap across the face, Tony yelled, "Shut your fuckin' face Botto."

Tony walked closer to Mr. Lonnegan aiming the gun at his head. "You see Charlie," he said nodding toward the sitting Charlie. "Charlie's got a reason to hurt you but I'm gonna save him to hurt Billy if I DON'T GET. . MY. . . FUCKIN'. . . MONEY aaaannndd I'm gonna save your bat for Charlie sos he got somethin' to use cause it looks like his arm ain't gonna be good for a while. Now I'd advise you to get the fuck outta my face."

Mr. Lonnegan backed off and headed in the direction of his car still steaming, nose into the side of Tony's car.

"Uh, uh, asshole," Tony said. "Since my car ain't workin' I'm borrowin' yours. You walk."

Mr. Lonnegan changed direction and headed up the street calling back: "This ain't over punk. . . It ain't over by a long shot."

Tony turned to Joey: "Pretty good eh Joe? Ya want a ride?"

"Good Tony. I knew you had it in you. Thanks but I'll walk. No offense. I think I've had enough excitement for one night."

"No offense taken counselor. Thanks for your help. Send me a bill. Good to see ya," Tony said with a smile and a wink. "Nicky you gotta drive me back to my house, then drop Charlie off at the hospital," he ordered.

"Tony, he broke my fuckin' arm," Charlie cried through clenched teeth. "You let him go without a scratch."

Tony stood close to Charlie. "Charlie, just go with Nicky. Don't ever talk back to me in front of people again or I will cap ya. I don't give a fuck about your arm. I care about my money. Shut the fuck up and go with Nicky or I'll break your other arm." Tony ordered.

"Fuck that. I can take care of myself, Tony. Thanks a shit-load – for nothin'"

"See what I gottta put up with when I listen to you, Joey?"

Joey shook his head as Tony got into Lonnegan's car. "At least there's no charge Tony," he called out with a wave.

"Keep that in mind Joe. Some day that no charge may come in handy."

"I don't doubt that at all Tony. Not at all."

Jim had learned most of what had happened that night from Joe when he returned home. He had picked up other bits and pieces here and there from neighbors and friends. He had also learned that Billy had returned to the hospital for another months stay and two months of rehabilitation as the results of a fractured kneecap.

Jim knew that this was probably not the end of it.

Chapter 6
The Defense

Joe sat at defense table reviewing copies of the juror questionnaires. Gradually the courtroom filled all but to capacity, the only area not invaded being that beyond the waist high wall separating the gallery from the attorney's desks.

Carolyn had not appeared as of yet choosing instead to remain in her small office between the two court rooms on the eighth floor until the jury venire, the initial pool of jurors, were seated.

Bill sat quietly confident in his belief that his prejudices would not be discovered. Michael, his court house friend, had explained that if he left out the important stuff in the juror questionnaire and if he did not raise his hand in response to the judge's questions he stood a good chance of being seated.

In unknowing tribute to his deceit, Joe, having read Bill's questionnaire, set it aside as a likely prospect for selection. Bill appeared to be blue collar, hardworking, a family man, low to middle income, a local pub beer drinker who probably had a neighborhood bookie. The lack of criminal record most likely bespoke a drunk driving or disorderly person conviction after a Sunday afternoon football game barbecue.

Joe held little expectation that Bill would make the final cut. He and Carolyn both had the option of knocking off sixteen people from the potential jury for any reason. Joe's purpose for setting aside Bill was twofold; he was attracted solely by the questionnaire and was inherently distrustful of its circumspection. As it sat apart from the larger group yet to be reviewed, it reminded Joe of its existence and its lack of total disclosure.

As the day wore on the largest number of people seeking release were excused because of the gruesome details of Tommy Francone's death. They would have to view startling 8 by 10 color glossies showing the deceased tied to the pier and his systematic dissection at autopsy. Not many had the stomach for this type of expose and the court was generally unwilling to take the chance that a juror would become physically sick during the trial or inform him that they could not continue.

It took four long days to select the final sixteen that would sit in judgment of Tony. Bill made the final cut, Carolyn preferring the save her last preemptory challenge for Antonio Feducci of the North End of Boston.

Joe certainly was not smug about the jury. It was probably as good a jury as any especially in light of the fact that Tony had been labeled as Mafia by every newspaper, magazine, television and radio for the last ten years. In this case a jury was a jury. When it came right down to it no matter what the law was and no matter how many times the jury would be told to apply it they would, of course, decide with their hearts. Intelligence seldom won the battle with emotions. Luckily, the fourth and last day of selection was Friday. This would give Joe and Carolyn the opportunity over the weekend to prepare their opening statements and their examinations of the first batch of witnesses.

After the close of court, Joe met again with Tony:

"What do you think of your jury?" Joe asked an unusually quiet defendant.

"Shit Joe, it don't matter," Tony answering dejectedly. "The bastards got me just where they want me. I've had my balls in a sling ever since I was arrested. No jury's gonna let me go anywhere but to the can."

"Tony you knew that all along. All I can do is the best I can, focus in on a couple of jurors, and try to go for a hung jury. I've seen worse situations and gotten good results. It's not over yet."

"What's the chance the judge'll kill the case?"

"I can't tell you that now Tony. Usually if the judge directs an acquittal it's based on something that does or doesn't develop during the trial. It is very seldom that the Commonwealth will go forward on a case that won't get over the rail. We'll just have to wait until the close of their case."

"Well let's hope that they don't do shit, cause' I wouldn't give myself the odds I've given on the street my whole life. And believe me that ain't saying much."

"I know Tony, I know," Joe said sympathetically. "If you need anything over the weekend call me at home. I talked to your mother and aunt and they'll be up to see you on Saturday and Sunday so you'll have some company."

"Joe, you think you can get me up to the dorm? General pop really sucks." Tony was referring to the upper tier of the Charles Street jail that is more reminiscent of a college dormitory as opposed to the single cells that run along the sides of the tiers on the lower floors.

"I can call the Sheriff but I doubt it," Joe said. "Number one they don't like you and number two they don't want to expose you to any more people than is absolutely necessary. They're worried you'll put a hit out on the C.I."

"You know Joe; they treat this whole fuckin' thing like it's the Godfather Five!"

Joe looked at Tony and shrugged a little without a word. He put his large hands on Tony's knee and said, "I'll see you on Monday. I'll be here at about eight o'clock if you don't need me before then. Try to relax."

Joe left lockup waving good night to the court officers. While he knew that Monday would be the first day of a potential three week trial that probably would hold surprises for both defense and prosecution, he could not know that Sunday would be the first day of eternity for one other caught up in the whirlwind of the Domainio infamy.

Chapter 7
Death Follows

The 14th floor maid at the Bradford Hotel had knocked at seven in the morning, later at ten, and now a six that same evening. Earlier, as she did now, she had called out, "Maid!" Ted had called back, "Don't need ya!" This time, at six, Fred called out in frustration, "Come back in an hour!"

Fred had become progressively irritated with cleaning the four-room suite. For the past two weeks he had played cleaning lady, roving throughout kitchen, living room, and bedrooms, picking up after Ted and the C.I. He wasn't a clean freak by any means, his car a testament to his own lackadaisical attitude about filth, but he didn't have to live in his car. He had to live here. He had taken the initiative early during their now two-week stay and it appeared he was locked in. Oh, they were conscious enough to roughly stack their dishes on the living room table - a kind of appeasement to the mystery cleaning elf - but it was clear that they either had no qualms about how they lived or were happy with the services of Freddy the maid.

Irritated to the point of madness Fred had decided, even before the maid's early morning knock, that he was at the end of his patience. After Ted's second rebuke, he took a demonstrative stand refusing to play kitchen housewife anymore. Since ten o'clock that morning he had let the dishes stack in the kitchen hoping that the smell of rotted food would motivate Ted to pitch in. Instead, upon complaint, Ted commented: "If you don't want to clean it, just leave it. It don't bother me." The C.I. on the other hand was much more philosophical. "I'm the one that's gotta take the stand and put my life on the line," he boasted prideful. "I ain't becoming no maid for a couple of babysitters. If you don't like the mess, you clean it. Personally, I don't give a shit."

When the maid returned at seven, Fred had had enough. "Open the door and let her in for Christ sakes," he demanded. "I'm tired of this bullshit."

"Look Fred, I'm not breakin' procedure just cause' you're Felix Unger of District A."

"Fuck you Ted. I'll escort her through the whole place. I won't leave her side. She can clean up a little, do the fuckin' dishes, strip the beds. Christ she can leave the sheets and I'll make the beds."

"Let 'er in," the C.I. chimed, "then she'll kill me and then you guys and then we won't need no clean sheets except for what they bury ya in."

"Look I'm lettin' her in. You guys can go to hell."

Fred was at the door and had it half opened before Ted could react. In a split second, muttering an incredulous "Shit!", Ted was up, across the room, and standing in front of the now fully opened door, gun drawn, crouched in a combat stance.

In the hallway behind a cart filled with detergents and cleaning paraphernalia stood one very frightened maid. When she saw Ted and the gun she froze babbling rapidly, "I'm leavin', I'm leavin', don't shoot please, I ain't never seen nothin', just let me go."

Ted lowered his gun with a roll of his eyes. "It's all right. We're police officers," Fred said showing her his badge. Reaching for his wallet he said quickly, "Don't worry. No ones gonna hurt you. We just need you to clean up a little. Look we'll pay you extra."

"You mean you'll pay her extra," Ted added.

Fred waved Ted silent while he opened his wallet and selected a ten dollar bill. "Look, here's ten bucks," Fred offered with outstretched hand. "Just pick up the trash and leave some towels and clean sheets." A little more than hesitant about mentioning the kitchen for fear that it would blow the deal Fred pleaded instead, "It won't take you more than ten minutes. Come on. No ones gonna hurt ya. Ted here didn't mean nuthin'. Its just procedure to pull his piece like that whenever we open the door."

The maid looked at Fred suspiciously and asked timidly, "What's goin' on here? Why're here? Is this some kinda stakeout?"

"Ya, that's right," Fred agreed. "A stakeout. Nuthin' dangerous goin' on. Whadd'ya say? Just a little cleaning."

The maid looked at the ten dollar bill, pushed the cart part way through the door and peered into the room spotting the C.I. as Ted moved protectively closer to him. She rolled the cart in further, past Fred, took the bill and expressed wide-eyed amazement at the condition of the living room. "Ten bucks," she exclaimed. "This is gonna cost more like twenty. Jesus, what the heck have ya been doing in here?"

Fred turned in time to see a smirk on Ted's face and the C.I. give a fool's chuckle.

"Okay, twenty Bucks. But you gotta hit the kitchen, that's the worst," Fred answered with false resignation seizing the opportunity to mention the kitchen. "Then you can move to the bedrooms, the bathroom, and then in here, and you're done."

The maid took the other ten dollar bill Fred had liberated from his wallet and pushed the cart past the small door and into the kitchen. Fred heard a groan as she disappeared around the corner.

"I still got the best of the deal," Fred said.

"Sure you did Fred. She just took you like a pro."

At the word 'pro', training clicked in Ted's mind - protocol. He looked at Fred for a second before he leapt around the corner into the kitchen. The maid, back to him, was closing the cabinet above the sink with one hand while reaching to turn on the kitchen faucet with the other. He stepped partially into the living room and through clenched teeth said in a whisper: "I thought you said you'd escort her around the place asshole."

"Oh ya," Fred said guiltily. "Sorry."

The maid, in the company of Fred, moved from room to room grumbling at the mess and the supervision. She made no comment directly but her message was clear. She slammed the door when she left, a little more than noticeably upset.

The next morning Ted woke and while still dusted with sleep wandered into the kitchen. Approaching the sink he reached for a water glass in the cabinet above while at the same time viewing the immediate area below. He had to admit the kitchen was pretty clean. As he peered down the counter to his right, two glass jars, one filled with ammonia - the other with chlorine, set precipitously against the inside of the cabinet door, toppled over, exploding in the sink. When the two liquids mixed a gas formed, rapidly filling the kitchen with a cloud, overtaking Ted in the first few moments.

Ted didn't have a chance. The gas took his last half-breath. His lungs constricted, his diaphragm collapsed and he fell over backwards fracturing his skull on the floor. Fred and the C.I., sitting in the living room watching the news, heard the glass break and Ted fall. Instinctively they ran to help. Once inside the kitchen they were quickly overtaken by the fumes. Both Fred and the C.I. landed, stacked on top of dead Ted.

No maid came to clean that morning. After all, the hotel had given strict instructions to its staff, and, besides, the maid was prohibited from room 411.

The "maid" returned to Hanover, changed, and got ready for her shift. "If that don't get me noticed," she mumbled to herself, "Tony's blind." I ain't gonna end up fuckin' for money my whole life."

Chapter 8
The Prosecution

Matted with a forest of giant heating units surrounded by trails of rooftop wooden maintenance walkways, the view of the Suffolk County Courthouse outside Carolyn's window was prestigious. Her small office was situated between court room 8A and 8B at the end of the wide "H" shaped foyer of the eighth floor. It was a short walk to court every morning; out the door, ten steps to the right. Far from aesthetically impressive - no hard wood wainscoting around the walls, no expansive desk, no fine wooden cabinets - it was the four walls and the door that spoke of status. It was the office alone, with her secretary, almost; she shared support staff with one other D.A. across the hall that made her the envy of most of her peers.

"Come in," Carolyn directed to her door in her no-nonsense voice.

As she had expected the medical examiner, the state psychologist, and detective Sullivan entered her office. Carolyn noticed immediately that the detective who had told her about the inmate at Charles Street Jail was not present. She also knew and expected that

Doctor Ablow, the C.I.'s doctor, would not be present A doctor in private practice would not part from his duties unless commanded by the court to appear and reimbursed for his time. The medical examiner, on the other hand, for all intents and purposes, was an arm of the District Attorney's Office and as such was utilized as a liaison to the private sector. A request for the presence of the medical examiner was as close to an order as he would get. His job would be in jeopardy if he disobeyed.

Carolyn remained seated when they entered. Detective Sullivan took the initiative to empty two of the three chairs in front of her desk of the cluttered Domainio files. After everyone was seated Carolyn started by addressing Doctor Shepard.

"Doctor I realize that you are not the doctor for my witness, but I take it you've had a chance to talk with Doctor Ablow and can fill me in on the C.I.'s condition."

"Yes I have," Doctor Shepard said. "I just left Doctor Ablow. As I indicated on the phone we are working together closely on this matter. Apparently, our boy is not feeling too well. The only saving grace is that the two bottles broke in the sink. By the time the C.I.

72

had entered the kitchen - it looks like he was the last one in - a vast amount of the mixture had dissipated down the drain. It appears that he was least affected by the fumes. As a result Doctor Ablow believes he will manifest the fewest symptoms of neurological damage. Fred will remain seriously brain damaged with little hope of recovery. Doctor Ablow also anticipates that both survivors will suffer serious respiratory problems, like emphysema, for the rest of their lives. Fred will not regain use of his voice. His vocal chords were burned beyond repair. They will heal but the scarring is unavoidable. His voice at best will be limited to a whisper but he will be able to communicate as much as his mental ability will allow."

"Understood," Carolyn said. "I have all the sympathy in the world for Fred and Ted's family but my greatest most immediate concern must be the ability of the C.I. to testify in this case. What can you tell me about his recovery?"

"Doctor Ablow has indicated that at this point the extent of brain injury to your witness is unknown."

"Brain damage!" Carolyn exclaimed. "Doctor please don't tell me that the C.I. has suffered brain damage. That is not something I want to hear."

"Unfortunately that is exactly what I'm telling you. There doesn't seem to be any question that there will be some brain dysfunction. How much is unknown. Nor do we know what type of limitations will result "

"Damn!" Carolyn exclaimed again.

The room was silent.

"Okay," Carolyn said thinking out loud, "Doctor Ablow can't tell at this point how much damage there is and how the C.I. will be affected right?"

"Right," Doctor Shepard agreed.

"So as far as we know he could still be competent to testify."

"That may be true Carolyn but he's not awake yet and there is no telling when he will regain consciousness or if he will be able to speak when he does. Especially if his vocal chords have been damaged as much as Fred's."

"Look - these are all 'ifs' aren't they?" Carolyn asked half rhetorically. "Doctor Ablow has said that he was the least affected by the gas. Based upon that representation I am going to proceed as if he will be able to testify until I hear to the contrary. I'm not about to drop this case because that punk Domainio got at the witness."

Carolyn turned to detective Sullivan. "And speaking of Domainio, what can you tell me about this inmate?"

Detective Sullivan, 53 years old, hardened by thirty years on the force and now assigned to the much desired position of investigator for the homicide division of the D.A.'s office had waited patiently despite feeling slighted at having to take second seat to the medical examiner.

"This guy's name is Terry Mandrake. He's Officer Pratt's rat. First of all he's got a record as long as the Mass. Pike. They need Casey and Hayes Movers to haul it in every time he goes to court." Characteristically Sullivan colored his statements with colloquialisms. "He says he was sitting in the next booth at Charles Street when Domainio's aunt, Nichole Sarpuzzi, came into to see him on Sunday. These booths have walls that come to about a foot below the ceilin', half wood, half Plexiglas." He felt in necessary to explain the lay out knowing that district attorneys seldom see the inside of jails. "You can hear quite a bit of what's bein' said in the booths near you. I checked the visitor sheet. It looks like Terry could've been in that area at the same time as Domainio for about five minutes."

"Detective you are aware that the hit was on Sunday morning, aren't you?"

"Ya I know that counselor but this visit was before the hit."

"How do you know that?" Carolyn asked.

"I just know it. Believe me when I tell ya it was before the hit," Sullivan answered a little annoyed.

Carolyn bristled at the condescending tone in the detective's voice. She hated these old boys. Setting aside the insult for the moment Carolyn asked for specifics.

"Do you have an initial report or statement detective?"

"No report. We didn't want to have anything you'd have to give Joe Balliro." He stopped and looked at Carolyn with more than a hint of condescension in his voice. "It's simple. He says he heard Domainio arrange the hit. What does it matter how he says it? He'll say it."

Carolyn had enough. Placing her hands over her eyes, elbows resting on her desk she asked scathingly: "What are you giving him in return for this 'truthful' testimony?"

"Nothin'," Sullivan responded.

"Detective, I'm not fucking around here. What is this guy in jail for and what did you promise him? I'm not an idiot. He's not going take the stand and testify against Tony Domainio unless he gets something from you. Now what did you promise we'd do?"

Sullivan let out a sigh of exasperation. What a pain in the ass this broad was, he thought. Why couldn't they have given this case to a man with experience?

"Okay, counselor. I'm just trying to help. When I said nothing I meant he won't blow it by testifying we made a deal. If he does there won't be a deal. It's standard procedure. He won't give it away."

"What's he in for and what are you offering him?" Carolyn repeated.

With another sigh and a slight throaty growl, Sullivan said: "He's in for armed assault with intent to rob, armed assault with intent to commit murder, assault and battery with a deadly weapon, breakin' and enterin' in the nighttime with intent to commit a felony, malicious destruction of property, and larceny over. The victim's over sixty-five. He's a third time offender."

"Jesus detective! What do you think Joe Balliro will do with that? There's no way a jury is going to believe we haven't cut a deal! This guys a maniac! Is he a druggy?"

"Yep."

"Is he related to Charles Manson?" Carolyn said hoping to rile the old detective. "What did you promise him - the street?" she continued.

Carolyn's last remark put Sullivan over the edge. With low voice and deliberation in his tone, Sullivan launched into a diatribe. "Hey, I come in here tryin' to help and you bust my balls. I got this guy that will testify that that piece of shit put a contract on the C.I. that ended up killin' one cop and making a veg out of the other. All I get from you is crap. If you don't want him, say so. Otherwise let me the fuck outta here. I've got a funeral to go to."

"Calm down detective," Carolyn said with conciliation. "We are all upset here."

"Upset," Sullivan added. "Upset! I got dead cops and you want to try and prove you're a man. Well be a man and take what I got or leave me the fuck alone."

"Look, that's it officer," Carolyn answered quickly. "You just quiet down. I'm not going to take any of that old boy, chauvinistic garbage. If you don't like that, you can leave. I just get a little perturbed when you're not straight with me. I'm not one of the 'old boys' that likes to read between the lines so he can act cagey when asked a question later. This case is too important and the pressure on me is too great. I want Domainio just as bad as everyone else. But I'm not going to have this case thrown out after Joe Balliro rips this rat to shreds on the stand. As it is, I may not be able to use him. More than likely he won't be permitted to take the stand. This stuff is the basis for additionally charges against Domainio. It does nothing to help my case except make it more interesting for the jury. You got that."

"I've been a cop for over thirty years," Sullivan responded still angry. "I understand more than you will ever know. If you want Mandrake, you let me know and we'll take care of it. That's all I got to say."

Seeing that Sullivan wouldn't back off, Carolyn decided to pull rank. "I want a report and a statement by Mandrake on my desk by five o'clock tonight. Do you have anything else for me?"

"No." Sullivan stood, addressed Doctor Shepard and the state psychologist, ignored Carolyn, and left the office in a huff. The air of combativeness disappeared behind a mild slam of the door.

Carolyn turned to Doctor Shepard. "Doctor I hate to do this to you but it is also absolutely necessary that I get a full report on the C.I.'s condition from Doctor Ablow by the end of the day. It is my hope that by then we will see some positive development in his condition. In fact, if he wakes before then I would appreciate a call."

"No problem Carolyn," Doctor Shepard said in earnest. "If I can be of any other help, please call."

"Doctor Bigalow," Carolyn said directing her attention to the psychologist who had remained silent up to now, "I'm sorry to have dragged you out here for nothing. I hoped you had the opportunity to talk to the C.I. Obviously that's not the case."

Doctor Bigalow was an exceptional and gentle professional having all the attributes necessary to heal emotional wounds. Recognizing the distrust generated by detective Sullivan and noting telltale signs of stress in Carolyn's voice and manner, he sought to assure her of his integrity.

"In all honesty, Carolyn, there's not much I can do in any event. My sense is that if you tell the court that I have been utilized to evaluate the patient you'll only harm your case. In any event, I could only be of help if the damage the patient suffered resulted in some behavioral manifestation that is linked to a neurological source. If it turns out any injury is non-specific, you won't need my services."

"I understand Doctor. It was my hope that you could compare the extent of injury of the officer with that of the C.I. and indicate to me whether or not the damage caused some additional psychological trauma that would impact on his competency or hinder his ability to communicate."

"If your witness survives, there is bound to be some residual emotional trauma that could rise to a level of Post Traumatic Stress Disorder or some variant of a Dissociative Disorder," Dr. Bigalow explained carefully, "but given your witnesses violent background, I can't say I am to confident it can be diagnosed. This type of personality is generally pathological. Underlying pathology this deep could mask any emotional injury secondary to the attempt on his life. Characteristically the reaction would be to avenge the wrong."

"So he could be the same kind of guy he was before the injury?" asked Carolyn.

"He could be. He could be more violent. He could be passive. It's unknown at this point," responded the Doctor. "

"Ok. Guess he's a blank right now. Can I call on you if I need you, Doctor?"

"Absolutely," Doctor Bigalow agreed.

"Thank you both for your time," Carolyn ended while standing. "I've got a big day in court tomorrow. The more information I have, the better for the case."

After both men left Carolyn sat down at her desk and set to the task of preparing for Tuesday morning. The rest of Monday was lost in a bed of concentration, consultation, and composition.

Chapter 9
The Defense

When Joe arrived in courtroom 8B on Monday morning Carolyn was waiting. As she walked towards him with obvious purpose, wound up tight for business, he took the initiative to speak first in an effort to avoid any possible harangue.

"This couldn't be about what I read in the paper this morning could it?"

"Good guess counselor," Carolyn answered. "I've asked for a conference with the judge," an obvious hardness in her voice. "He's ready when we are."

"Let's go," Joe said willingly.

Even a passing glance at the papers that morning would have apprised the casual onlooker of the latest development in the Domainio murder case. Joe, expecting some coverage given that opening statements were scheduled to start that morning, eagerly recovered the papers from his front step. As he unfolded both publications he spotted the banner headlines reading them with guarded disbelief.

MOB HIT ON MAJOR STATE WITNESS IN DOMAINIO CASE !!

and.

KEY WITNESS IN DOMAINIO CASE SUBJECT OF MOB STYLE HIT!!

Even a cursory review of the stories following made it obvious that opening statements would not start that morning. First Amendment explosions often delayed trial.

Now in court, with a file that had suffered the hurried dissection of an unexpected light day, Joe stood at the entry to chambers a little unsure of what to anticipate.

In chambers Judge Wilton brought the matter up to speed without fanfare expressing his irritation at the unavoidable delay the Bradford hit was expected to cause. "Good morning counselors. Miss Cheline I take it your request for this conference involves your C.I. What is his status?"

"Good morning your Honor," Carolyn said, careful to greet the justice before answering. "As the court is aware the C.I., the Commonwealth's key witness, was the subject of a mob contract hit last night..."

"Wait a minute," Joe automatically jumped in. "Your Honor, I object not only to the Commonwealth's characterization that last night was some kind of contract hit but also to the inference that my client had anything to do with it."

"I didn't say anything about your client Mr. Balliro," Carolyn said directing her comments to Joe.

"Oh come on Carolyn that was clearly your inference," Joe responded.

Carolyn, already exposed to a long night at the Bradford Hotel - suite 1411 - pressure from her boss, co-workers, as well as every cop from Chief to beat, slipped her composure and with heavily laced anger lashed out at Joe. "Look I've got one officer dead and another who might as well be, and I've got someone at the jail who will testify that he heard your client order the hit on the C.I. The last thing I need is your attitude about his innocence."

Joe didn't respond satisfied that he had gotten the desired effect and knowing full well the judge would not permit discourse between the attorneys in his presence.

"Okay, okay," Judge Wilton refereed. "Carolyn you want to tell me exactly what you have? It appears I'm the only one who doesn't know what's going on here and I'm not in the mood to second guess anybody."

Carolyn took a minute to regain her composure. "Your honor," she began calmly. "I have a witness who will testify that he heard the defendant instruct a visitor, his aunt Nichole Sarpuzzi, at the Charles Street Jail to get the confidential informant. Shortly thereafter a murderer in the guise of a maid entered the suite and planted a device that killed one of the finest and most decorated police officers on the force."

I earning through sources that morning that one of the officers was dead, the other crippled, and the C.I. unconscious, Joe had been able to supplement the sketchy and contradictory information from the Herald and Globe and even had been able to learn that the Commonwealth had something or someone that connected all this to Tony, but he had not be able to determine who or were that person was. Carolyn just told him. There was a rat at the jail.

"Carolyn," Judge Wilton interrupted noticeably irritated at her vacillation, "what is the status of your witness?"

"One police officer is dead," Carolyn said determined to present her case staged in the most damning light, "the other is probably so badly brain damaged that he will never reach above a sixth grade level again. Fortunately, the witness is fine."

A moment passed before Judge Wilton realized with frustration that Carolyn did not intend to continue. "Counselor, you had better explain what happened in support of your assertion that your witness is capable of contributing to these proceedings."

"Your honor, I don't think I am required to do that under the rules. Mr. Balliro is not entitled. Especially in light of what has happened."

"Most respectfully your Honor," Joe responded. "I object to that statement. Firstly, my sister has indicated that she will offer another informant to point the finger at my client. Secondly, my sister blatantly suggests that my client and myself, either knowingly or unknowingly, had a hand in the death and injuries of the officers."

"If it's her intention to make this incident part of her case I'm entitled to all the Commonwealth has. I motion to the Court for an order compelling discovery about all that occurred at the hotel and the inmate informant."

"Denied, in part, at this time Mr. Balliro." Turning to address Carolyn, Judge Wilton said: "Carolyn you had better tell me why you believe that your key witness can still testify. I've been led to believe that without him you don't have a case. If I'm forced to acquit the defendant because the C.I. could not take the stand or took the stand and obviously was incompetent the only happy people in the court will be Mr. Balliro and his client. Believe me it won't be a happy day for the District Attorney's office."

"Your honor may I know the extent of your partial granting of Mr. Balliro's motion to compel discovery so that I can tailor my comments?"

"Counselor," Judge Wilton after a sigh, "you are not to tailor your response. You are to give me a detailed account of what happened and the condition of the C.I."

"Okay your honor," Carolyn succumbed. "But please note my objection," she said directing her comments to the court stenographer busily taking a verbatim transcript.

"From what we are able to tell a person disguised as a maid was permitted to enter the suite where the C.I. was being held in protective custody. She planted two glass jars in a cabinet above the sink without the officers seeing her. One had chlorine in it, the other had ammonia. They were set against the inside of the door of the cabinet when it was closed.

In the morning one of the officers, the one now deceased, opened the cabinet above the sink for whatever reason. The jars fell, broke, and the ammonia and the chlorine mixed. The coroner tells me that the mixture of these two solvents creates a gaseous vapor that when inhaled at the very least will cause brain damage and at the greatest will cause death. The other officer ran in immediately afterward with the C.I. The three were found stacked together on the floor of the kitchen by additional officers that were dispatched to the location when the B.P.D. did not receive a 10:00 a.m. check-in call."

Joe restrained the urge to ask the next obvious question instead drawing lines on a yellow legal pad at the end of the last paragraph of scribbled notes.

Judge Wilton asked once again: "What's the condition of your witness?"

"He'll be able to testify," Carolyn responded curtly.

Judge Wilton, now resigned to cross examination said: "You said the officer has brain damage, didn't you?"

"Carolyn, instinctively hesitant to adopt a leading question said, "He'll be lucky to achieve, with therapy, a sixth grade level of education."

"And your witness is unconscious?"

"He's not awake yet."

"So it's your position that although not conscious you can represent to this court that he will be able to testify?"

"All I can tell your honor is that in my brief conversation with the medical care providers at the Massachusetts General Hospital they have assured me that he will most likely recover."

Judge Wilton tried again, "So you are taking the position that he will be able to testify, right?"

Absolutely," Carolyn said.

Turning to Joe the Judge prompted: "Mr. Balliro?"

"I move that the court conduct a competency evaluation of the confidential informant."

Carolyn reacted immediately: "Opposed most strenuously."

"The basis for your objection counselor?"

"Your honor the defendant cannot be told the identity of the C.I. let alone be allowed to view him on the stand in open court and I would object to Mr. Balliro being given the opportunity to question the witness before he testifies in front of the jury."

"I'll waive his presence your honor," Joe offered.

"Wait a minute," Judge Wilton interjected. "I'm not going to allow a defendant in a trial of this magnitude to waive any of his rights. In addition, Miss Cheline, you have indicated to me that you intend to offer an inmate at the Charles Street jail to testify that the defendant ordered the attack on the C.I. That says to me that you are accusing the defendant of knowing who the C.I. is and ordering his death, otherwise how could you support any allegation that Mr. Domainio did anything?"

"The Commonwealth is entitled to protect the integrity of its informants," Carolyn said stalling for time to calculate a viable response. "On that basis alone that defendant should not be allowed to examine the witness prior to his testimony at trial." Losing her train of thought she strayed from the issue of the C.I.'s competency to that of whether the defendant was entitled to hear the C.I.'s testimony before trial. "Furthermore your honor," Carolyn continued getting back on track, "I stated earlier that I had an inmate who heard the defendant order the C.I. killed. I didn't say that the defendant ordered the hit by name. Therefore, should the defendant not know the C.I.'s name it would be very dangerous to let him know now, especially when one attempt has been made on his life, and he is now in a location far less secure than the hotel."

At the drop in Carolyn's voice Joe began his opposition. "Your Honor here we have the classic case of splitting hairs. On the one hand the Commonwealth would have you believe that the defendant ordered the hit on the C.I. while on the other hand they say he doesn't know who the C.I. is. According to the Commonwealth somebody must know who the C.I. is. The cat is out of the bag. Furthermore, the issue isn't whether the defendant has a right to hear the testimony of the C.I. before trial; it is whether the C.I. is competent to testify. As your honor is aware this is a very narrow issue that can be answered without delving into a substantial amount of his actual trial testimony. I think your honor recognizes the import of not only the Commonwealth's allegations that the defendant had something to do with this incident but also the assertion that the C.I. is unscathed. We have been told that one police officer is dead and the other has serious irreversible brain damage."

"In the face of all these revelations this morning it is clear that I am entitled to all medical records of the officers and the C.I.; I am entitled to have an expert examine these records; I am entitled to have an expert examine the surviving officer and to review the autopsy report and the physical evidence of the deceased officer; and I am entitled to have this Court determine if the C.I. has the ability to recall, recant, and relate his observations when he testifies. This court and the defendant ought not to be exposed to a long trial only to discover that the key witness for the Commonwealth is no longer available. All these concerns far outweigh the interest of the Commonwealth in protecting the integrity of the Witness Protection Program."

"I have to agree with Mr. Balliro counselor," Judge Wilton said to Carolyn. "Frankly, I can't see how you can represent to me that the witness is competent when you have one officer dead, another seriously injured, and an unconscious witness. I'm afraid you are going to have to show me that your witness is capable. I'm not going to waste this court's time and the public's money on a case that hinges on a person exposed to a gas that has caused so much damage."

"In the alternative your honor," Carolyn said, "would the court be willing to accept a complete report from the attending physician and the medical examiner before the court makes a final decision? I could have it for you in the morning."

"I would object to that your honor," Joe said.

"No," Judge Wilton said to Carolyn. "I am not going to expose this witness to the jury based solely on a medical report and face the prospect of a stinging cross examination by Mr. Balliro. I am simply not going to be put in the position of having to grant a mistrial or directed verdict." Leaning forward he advised, "Carolyn you have got to weigh your options. The admissibility of the testimony of the inmate informant is questionable at best. In any event he won't carry your case even if I allow him to take the stand. But I do not want to address that issue at this time. You have got to decide first if you will be willing to present the C.I. for a competency evaluation. Otherwise drop the case and pursue some other avenue."

Attempting to avoid at all costs the opportunity for Joe to examine the C.I. before the jury was present, Carolyn sought desperately a way to convince Judge Wilton to postpone his decision in the hope that she could more fully develop her argument against Joe's motion and perhaps even submit a memorandum in opposition. As it stood now not only had she been unsuccessful at convincing the Judge to proceed with trial, Joe had been successful at establishing her case as a one witness parade; a disadvantageous and unadvisable characterization of any case. With no roads to travel Carolyn wisely relied on a tried and true technique in support of her request. Shifting from the singular to the plural, Carolyn sheltered herself under cover of the Office of the District Attorney and the people for which it stands.

"It has always been the position of the Commonwealth that we have a very strong case against the defendant. The C.I. was, I mean is, the focal point of the trial but we are confident that we can proceed successfully without him if necessary. However before we commit ourselves either way I would at least like to have the day to speak to my investigators and evaluate the Commonwealth's options."

"Granted," Judge Wilton ordered pleased to come to some conclusion that morning. "This day is not lost. I've got work to do. I'm going to bring down the jury and dismiss them for the day. We will adjourn until tomorrow morning. At that time I will expect some answers."

"Understood," echoed both counsel.

Joe followed Carolyn out of chambers. The courtroom was closeted with spectators and media. Having waited these past 45 minutes for some television type courtroom drama, they were anxious for any activity. As Joe and Carolyn and the court officers entered, the room quieted.

When the judge excused the jury with the appropriate instructions a noticeable groan was heard from the gallery, a groan that followed the crowd as the room emptied; the media waiting in the hall for comment, the spectators waiting to overhear.

In the quiet of the now almost empty courtroom and after Tony had been taken out by the officers, Joe approached Carolyn. "I'll be back in my office if you want to talk. We should communicate before tomorrow so we can provide the judge with some coordinated schedule in the morning."

"If that's a pitch for lesser time from the Commonwealth you can forget it," Carolyn said with distaste.

Joe stood for a moment, disappointed with her response. "Carolyn I'm just trying to be cordial and professional. It wasn't a pitch." With just a hint of frustration he said: "You know I've been around for a long time. I've taken a lot of punches and I've never blamed anyone whose fist I didn't see coming - good lesson to learn."

Carolyn ignored Joe's gratuitous advice and continued: "I've got a lot to do today Joe. If I need you I'll call you. Otherwise, you'll just have to take your surprises like I've had to."

"If you let me know what position you are going to take before tomorrow morning it will simply make for a more pleasant and efficient day."

"That's easy Joe," Carolyn said with spite, "I can tell you that right now. Expect that I will take the worse possible position for your client. There - no surprises."

Carolyn turned and walked away. Joe stared after her shaking his head.

In the holding cell Joe and Tony dealt with the expectations of a much weakened case and fell into reminiscence.

Joe long ago had separated experiences from Tony. Their shared memories now consisted of times together long ago and knowledge of events in the not so distant past learned from different perspectives at different moments from different sources.

Tony sat in silence looking as dejected as he had on Friday.

Although Joe never took his client's word for full value offered, he believed Tony when he said he had not ordered the hit on the C.I. Tony would have been much more enthused over Carolyn's predicament had he been responsible for these recent developments. He read Tony's silence as anger at the prospect of another inmate taking the stand against him - right or wrong. Tony had no tolerance, no understanding, and no power over someone who turned rat. To him, and many others within and without the criminal world, a rat was lowly and despicable.

"It's not like the old days anymore," Tony said quietly. "Shit, it's not like it was five years ago. Nobody's got any pride anymore Joe. It's got real dirty, real dirty."

Joe didn't respond.

"Ya know I sit in this place, it ain't so bad. Course' I'd like to get out of here but I can hack it. Ya be a man, you take your licks. You don't go fucking somebody else up just because you're some pussy." Tony stopped for a moment trying to think of an example of what he meant. Tino came to mind.

"Remember Tino, Joe? What a fuckin' waste. Some guy and him get in a beef over a fucking parking space. The guy pulls out a knife and sticks Tino right through the fucking heart. Tino's dead before he hits the ground."

"Ya I remember Tino's funeral. Somebody on Hanover Street told me he had died."

"Ya think the cops do anything about it? Nah. Just another guinea killing one of his own. I find out who did in six hours. The guy comes to me and apologizes. That's what I mean Joe. The guy was stand up. He knew I'd probably whack him right there but he comes to me and says, 'Tony I did a bad thing and I can't fix it. I gotta family,' he says. 'Ya understand Tony, I gotta family.' 'Ya well,' I says to him, 'Tino had a family too. Now they've got no father. So now you have two families. Because now you have to take care of Tino's.' The guy thanks me. He fuckin' thanks me Joe for not capping him right there on Fleet Street."

"Ya know that guy's been good all along and he's still being good while I'm in here. Tino's wife gets the money and thinks it comes from me. I didn't tell her. Why'd she have to know? She thought Tino was made and that's why I take care of her. And she thinks I capped the guy. Everybody's happy. What was I going do, Joe? Make another fuckin' widow and whack the guy? Put the family on welfare so the state can fuck them up?"

"Now Whadd'ya think the cops would have done if they knew it was this guy that capped Tino? They would'a put that guy up for life, the family on welfare, and no justice for Tino. Ya think Tino would care if they put this guy in jail? No, he just cared about his family. That's what so fucked up about this system, Joe, See what I mean. They do whatever the fuckin' want and say they're better than me. That's fuckin' bullshit. And then they used some fuckin' wimp asshole LIKE THIS RAT MutherFUCKER when they KNOW he's lying cause' THEY put him up to it."

As Tony's voice got louder Joe interrupted, "I understand Tony but take it easy. Everybody can hear you." Joe said pointing his thumb towards the officers on the holding area. "The last thing we need is another Commonwealth witness."

Tony was standing now, visibly upset. "FUCK the RAT, FUCK this PLACE, FUCK the JAIL, FUCK THE LAW, AND FUCK THE MOTHERFUCKER THAT THINKS HE'S GONNA RAT ON ME!"

"Great Tony, great," Joe said, "are you going to take my advice and quiet down or should I just invite the whole dock in here to take notes?"

Tony leaned forward and in a much quieter and restrained voice said: "You know Joe, they wanna say that I hit someone then I'll be happy to oblige. Then I swear to God, I'll shit on them from heaven, I don't give a fuck how far down in hell they are. They know this guy's a lyin' rat but they don't care they just wanna make their case. His death will be on their hands not mine."

"I hope you've gotten that out of your system Tony," Joe said. "Now you listen to me. You don't do anything but sit here like a good boy until the trial is over. If you do anything that ends up harming anybody I won't be able to protect you. We may have an attorney-client privilege but as far as I'm concerned as soon as you tell me that you are going to start trouble that privilege is in jeopardy. Frankly, if you were my friend you wouldn't put me in that position."

"Joe, it won't be no trouble at all."

"Tony I don't want to hear it. You've paid me for my advice and you're a friend. I'm warning you to behave yourself."

"Ya, ya Joe," Tony said slyly after a short pause. "Forget what I said. I was just blowin' off steam. I ain't gonna do anything except what you say, sit here and be a good boy and wait until the trial is over."

Joe wasn't convinced. Tony wasn't sincere. Rats never lived.

Chapter 10
A Juror and a Connection

Bill returned to South Boston angry at the delay. He had been brought into the courtroom with the jury at about 10:30 a.m., already fiercely irritated over having to wait for an hour and a half in a hot room with a bunch of idiots. He had expected some excitement. What he got were two bickering attorneys and a room full of news hounds. Once in his seat, Bill had concentrated on listening to the conversations between the court and the attorneys as they discussed not so quietly at 'side bar'. The jury had been told these matters were not for their ears but that did not apply to him. Nevertheless, he took care not to have it appear as though he was listening. Besides, it distracted him from staring at Domainio.

Although Bill could not hear all of what was being said, he could tell that there was heated discussion between counsel. Especially so for the D.A. who was very animated. Several times he saw the judge look over to the jury while telling her to keep her voice down. Bill could hear that.

After the attorneys had finished at side bar, the judge turned and excused them for the day. He explained to Bill and the others that matters necessitated their adjournment and that this good fortune would permit them a fresh start in the morning. Bullshit.

He gave them explicit instructions to avoid any publication or broadcast about the day's events.

Fuck you.

He told Bill and his fellow jurors that they should not speculate at what had occurred and should go home and enjoy the remainder of the day.

Crap.

Bill's anger was fueled by Judge Wilton's pleasant, fatherly, friendly, condescending, and pompous delivery. This aggravated his basic hatred, putting him in an even more foul mood.

Once in the hallway of the juror room upstairs Bill complained to co-juror Nancy Wilcock: "Why the hell did they bring us in there if they weren't gonna let us hear anything?"

"We're not supposed to talk about the case," Nancy responded.

"Jesus, I'm not talking about the case, I'm just askin' a question."

"Well, I'd appreciate it if you kept your comments to yourself. I, for one, wish to abide by the Judge's orders."

Christ, Bill thought, this one's a real pleasure. "Fuck this," Bill murmured. He was eager to get back to Southie and have a few beers.

When Bill turned up "A" street he saw Shawnessy at the ice house on the corner of 1st. He honked his horn. Patrick Shawnessy looked up and waved him over to the side of the road. Even though Bill lowered the passenger window, Patrick opened the door and sat next to him.

"What's goin' on Bill? Why ain't ya at work?" Patrick asked.

"I'm on the jury in the Domainio trial."

"Oh yea, I heard that. What's it like?"

"Like shit right now. The asshole lawyers can't get their shit together so we can get on with it."

"Have you seen Domainio yet?"

"Yea the punk's been at the defense table every time they bring us in."

"He's one bad dude," Patrick said. "Do me a favor and nail his ass for me."

"Happy to oblige. He's nothing but a punk. I'll be happy when they nail his ass to the wall for my own pleasure."

"Whadd'ya doing now?"

"Goin' home. I gotta wait for the kids to get out of school," Bill said looking for an excuse to get Patrick out of the car.

"Yea? Okay. Well, I'll see ya round. I gotta watch the ice house for Teddy. I'll be here for a while if ya want to go out for a couple pops later."

"Okay, maybe, I'll see ya later," Bill said shifting the car from drive to neutral and back to drive again. "Take care."

With lessening hope of finding anyone he might consider wasting the day with, Bill decided to go home, watch the 12:00 o'clock news and find out what he wasn't supposed to know. The trip home was short but distant enough to allow Bill's thoughts to drift to thoughts of his father.

Bill had been in the car, his leg in a cast. Even though they had paid the money, and Bill had been out of the hospital for a week without another broken leg, he knew Domainio was still after his father. Tony wouldn't settle for money alone. His image had been damaged and one of his men injured, but his dad said he would show that guinea who's boss.

As they sat at a light on Hanover Street, somebody came over to the car and smashed his father's arm as it rested on the driver's side door, window down. Bill heard the pop of a muffled handgun. His father grabbed his stomach, a bullet lodged deep in his intestine. He opened the car door and fell into the street. He lay there, squirming, screaming, and no one, not one miserable guinea motherfucker, did anything to help. It had to be ten minutes before the ambulance arrived and by then his father was unconscious. The cops came after the ambulance - after! He's dead. He just died there. They did nothing. Blood everywhere. His body bloated. Lying on his side. Face down. Bill remembered his father's last breath, blowing bubbles in a pool of his own blood. He pisses and shits himself and he's dead - just like that, dead. I gotta tell my mother - it'll kill her - my dad. He just died there. Dad.

Worked up now, adrenaline flowing, tears in his eyes, Bill was so angry his skin temperature had risen several degrees. Without realizing it, he had hyperventilated as he became more agitated. This in turn caused him to become oxygenated which in turn calmed him down enough so that he could gain some semblance of control.

A loud blast of a horn brought him back. Wiping his eyes, he thrust his middle finger in his rear view mirror, pushed down hard on the gas and launched toward his apartment.

Inside his five-room apartment on 2nd Street Bill headed for the kitchen, opened the refrigerator, pulled out a stout, and grabbed a handful of sliced roast beef from a lunch plate left open on the lower shelf. As he was walking to the television room, Mary called out from the second floor: "Is that you Bill?"

No, Bill thought, it's the fuckin' boogie man. With his mouth half full of roast beef he grunted back: "Yea, it's me."

"You're home early."

A fuckin' brain surgeon, my wife, he thought. "They let us go early," he called back.

"How'd it go?"

"I don't wanna talk about it. The judge says I can't," Bill said, finding refuge in a previously ignored order.

Eager to eat and catch the news he flipped on the television and sat back while in the process of taking a large gulp from the stout. Spilling some beer on his shirt, he let out another curse as he set everything down on the stack table in front of the couch.

As he stood to wipe down the liquid and brush off any crumbs, the noon broadcast caught his eye and his jaw stopped in mid-gnaw, his mouth, full with roast beef, open in disbelief. He reached over and raised the audio on the television returning to the edge of his seat. If his kids had been there he would have slapped them quiet.

Although he knew there had been a hit at the Bradford Hotel he had no idea who had been hit and that they had someone who would say that Tony had ordered it. "Son of a bitch!" Bill exclaimed. "Mary," he hollered with a smirk. "Mary!!! You won't believe this!"

Bill stopped hollering just in time to learn that the judge had ordered that the inmate informant was not to testify. "I don't believe it," Bill said to no one. "Son of a BITCH!!!" He was yelling now. "WHO THE HELL DOES HE THINK HE IS!!!"

At that moment Mary came around the corner of the hallway with a worried look. "Bill, what's the matta'?"

"That son of a bitch judge thinks he came keep things from us? Well we'll see. We'll see."

"Bill what are you talking about?"

"That punk Domainio put the hit out on the guy that was gonna put the finger on him and that jerk judge has ordered that we don't get to hear it."

"Bill, I don't understand what you talking about," Mary said half turning in dismissal to go back to the kitchen.

Bill followed her. "Look Mary you heard how someone tried to kill the guy that was gonna testify against Domainio, right?"

"Yea everybody's heard that this mornin'"."

"I didn't," Bill said indignantly. "I do now. Well they got a guy that heard Domainio order him killed and that judge ain't gonna let us hear from him."

Mary took a minute to assimilate what Bill had said. Thinking for a moment, she came to a sudden revelation, turned from walking away and said: "Bill if you are not supposed to know about that, how come you're watching the news and know about it?"

"Look, Mary that ain't the point. They got a guy that will nail that punk and the judge thinks we're a bunch of kids that shouldn't outta know. That's a bunch of crap." Pausing for a moment, Bill boasted: "Well I know. It don't matter if they tried to hide stuff from me. I'M GONNA find out," Bill said with emphasis.

"Bill, that don't seem right," Mary said calmly recognizing Bill to be in one of his moods.

"I gotta a duty to perform Mary," Bill justified. "I took an oath. They picked me cause' they knew I'd do my duty and I intend to. No matter what they try and hide."

"I don't know Bill. Couldn't ya get in trouble violating the judge's order like that? Couldn't you go to jail?"

"Oh Jesus, Mary don't ya think I know what I'm doing. I knew that punk did that hit anyway. I'm just pissed off because they got a bunch of people on the jury that ain't as smart as me and probably haven't figured it out. I tell ya Mary I ain't gonna stand for it."

"Whadd'ya gonna do Bill?"

"I don't know. But I tell ya somebody ought to do something."

Bill returned to the couch to finish his stout periodically leaning forward to switch the television from channel to channel. I gotta do something, he thought. I gotta think of how to find out about this legit so I can tell the others. That's what I gotta do. I've got to think of a way I could have learned this that wouldn't get me in trouble. He thought about calling his friend Mike but he figured Mike would probably tell him to keep his mouth shut and do what the judge says. I have to blame it on somebody, he thought wildly. I've got to figure out who could of told me without getting anyone in trouble. There's gotta be a way.

Bill's logic was distinct and defiant. 'Fair' was that he should be treated with respect for his intelligence; 'justice' was that Tony Domainio be punished. He was different. There was no risk he would be tainted from exposure to matters outside the court and therefore no reason he should be restrained as if he were just another juror. The Commonwealth to which he had sworn an oath could be certain that he would do what was right - as any good citizen would.

Chapter 11
Just Business

Mandrake shook his head back and forth slowly while raising his middle finger at Sergeant Walsh.

He couldn't talk. They had cut him real good. Sergeant Walsh thought he looked a lot like the dead bodies you see on TV in them old cowboy movies, mouth sewn shut, propped up in a casket with a sign reading "Do you know this man?"

They had cut Mandrake's top and bottom lip lengthwise from end to end. He had 30 odd stitches running the whole length. He wouldn't be talking for a while.

"Yea, you're gonna testify or I'll break both your legs myself." Sergeant Walsh threatened.

Mandrake shook his head again motioning with his finger, the only part of his arm he could move.

He had been caught by two Bubbas in the laundry room pushed behind a big laundry drum out of sight. Domainio appeared from behind them.

"Ok. you fuck," Tony said ominously. "You're gonna tell me you ain't gonna talk, but I gotta make sure."

Mandrake pleaded.

One Bubba held him down on a small metal table, his head and arms hung over the edge. The other put a belt on his forehead and forced his head still, the top of his head facing the floor behind the table. Tony walked around the table and stood in front of Mandrake's face, a little lower than waist high to Tony. Tony took a piece of duct tape he had liberated from a piece of equipment in shop and taped Mandrake's mouth shut. Not to keep him quiet, but to keep his mouth still. Tony took a small blade made from a spoon stolen from the cafeteria and slowly cut open both his lips. Mandrake screamed. The noise of the laundry drowned him out. Blood filled his mouth and noise, gagging him. He vomited, the acid from his stomach burning his open wounds. The Bubba released the belt on Tony's command, but Mandrake was still restrained.

The Bubba that had released the belt moved to the side of the table and held out Mandrake's arm over the edge of the table. Tony began to exert slow pressure on the arm opposite the bend of the elbow. He took his time building up pressure until the elbow cracked loudly. Mandrake was almost out, but he still could be heard crying and moaning. Tony woke him up. He twisted the broken arm as if to try and tear it off. Mandrake screamed, spitting blood and squirming viciously. Tony moved to the other arm, repeating the lesson.

All three men began to beat Mandrake. They beat him unconscious around his thighs and groin. They didn't stop until they saw blood stain the crotch of his orange prison pants. They dragged his body to the front of the laundry drum, opened the door, and threw him in, shutting the door behind him.

Tony dropped the spoon into the floor drain. They left in separate directions.

Sergeant Walsh really didn't give a shit about Mandrake, he was breathing and that's all the Sergeant needed. With one more assurance to Mandrake that he would take the stand - or else - he left the jail.

He had a report he needed to write for that broad Cheline.

Chapter 12
Defense Planning

Rowes Wharf moved ever so slightly, an illusion created by the movement of the ocean and the sound of the water constantly slapping against the pier's concrete footings. Harbor Towers, however, did move. Well seated into Rowes Wharf, the two thirty story towers swayed back and forth some 6 degrees indiscernible to the eye, teased by the ocean's winds. Joe scanned the dolphin ship permanently moored to his right, his gaze roaming across the fifty or so sloops and smaller craft either docked at the base of the towers or anchored in the surrounding water access to the shore. He was lost in a daydream of sailing, teased ever so slightly by a salt water addiction that had captured millennia of hearts. The crystal blue sky, moderate temperature, sea breeze, and the wide berth of the plaza invited exhausted tourists to rest from the arduous task of sightseeing at the adjacent Long Wharf. It was their presence that jostled Joe back to shore and into Tower II.

Working near the ocean and within walking distance of most all of the courts in Boston, Joe enjoyed the lifestyle he had acquired from thirty years of labor in the courts of the Commonwealth. From the hardwood floors to the mid-wall to ceiling, wall to wall windows, his office on the twenty-second floor was a symbol of that achievement. When he stepped into the waiting area of his office, he was accosted by associates whose needs ranged from advice to curiosity. He accepted his messages from Brenda and Lois without comment, acknowledged Frank, and directed him into his office through the main floor facing out to the Harbor. Julianne, his daughter, and the three other associates in the firm followed. Having read the morning editions they were all anxious for greater detail.

"What's up?" Frank asked as he sat in one of the tufted chairs in front of Joe's desk. Julianne took the other. The others stood.

"Who do we have at Mass. General?" Joe asked.

"That's where the C.I. is," Frank stated more than asked, anticipating Joe's request. "I read it this morning. The paper said he wasn't hurt but that one of the cops croaked."

"Well that's what they'd have us believe but I think he's out of the running. Carolyn is taking the position that he'll be able to testify. I need to know just how bad he is."

"No problem," Frank said as he rose from his chair. "He's probably in intensive care. I've got someone in there that can give me the lowdown. Have for you in ten minutes."

"I need it yesterday," Joe said in all candor.

"Done," Frank called from outside the office.

"What does Tony say?" Julianne asked.

"Says he didn't do it," Joe said. "I believe him."

"Well it certainly is convenient for him," Julianne responded in disbelief.

"That's true. But that would be true in any set of circumstances. I don't think he did it, but he may take it on the chin anyway."

"What do you mean?'

"Carolyn says she's got an inmate rat that will point the finger at him."

Julianne smiled. "Christ Dad, don't you ever get a simple case without outrageous surprises!"

"There's no such thing daughter, no such thing," Joe said calmly.

Frank returned smiling like the military leader of a small Middle Eastern coup. "He's done Joe. He's lucky if he remembers his name. The guy's not even awake and it doesn't look like he'll be awake for another week."

"Who did you speak to?"

"Intensive care nurse. She's been on duty since they brought him in. They won't let her go home. Seems they don't have the greatest confidence in their ability to screen people," Frank chuckled.

"Did she tell you what happened?"

"Pretty much like the paper said. Some maid set up two bottles that fell into the sink. One with chlorine. One with ammonia. In the morning one of the cops went for a glass and boom! They fell into the sink, broke, the fluids mixed, and a deadly - and I mean deadly - gas filled the room. Killed one cop. The other is a mental cripple. Mr. X is unconscious. They think that because he's not awake he's hurt worse than the other cop that regained consciousness. Most likely took the deepest breath of the stuff. That's what the Doc thinks. That's not from the nurse."

"Remind not to clean my house," Julianne interjected. Turning to Frank she said, "They've got an inmate rat that says he heard Tony order the hit on the C.I."

Joe shook his head waving the rat off with one hand. "I'm not too worried about him. He's got to be insane to testify in this case. Besides Wilton won't let him take the stand. There's no basis for admission of his testimony. He won't want to create an appellate issue."

"Well she could argue that it's an admission of guilt on the part of Tony. By trying to kill the witness he's admitted that he's guilty," Julianne played devil's advocate. "Or she'll argue that it shows consciousness of guilt."

"It won't fly," Frank joined in. "Wilton won't want to create the issue unless he sees that the Commonwealth's case is falling apart and they need the rat."

"Unfortunately it looks like their case is falling apart," Joe mused.

"Is she going to argue it in the morning?" Frank asked.

"Well Wilton sent clear signals that he's not going to allow the inmate rat to testify but she was able to postpone his decision until tomorrow. I agree with you though, he might allow him to take the stand if her case is a mess. And I think he sees that already. He gave her an ultimatum; decide what she going to do with the C.I. and with her case. I may have pushed a little too far. I don't want that rat. I also requested a competency hearing on the C.I. Obviously she doesn't want to give me a crack at him but if I push it and Wilton's forced to give it to me he may decide that she needs the rat."

"What are you going to do?" Frank asked.

"Well we know now that Mr. X is at this point incompetent. How long he will remain that way we don't know, so we need updates on his condition. See if you can get periodic reports."

"Sure Joe. Not a problem," Frank assured.

"For now I'll have to proceed as though he won't be able to testify or at the least will be easy to cross. The best case scenario will be if Mr. X disqualifies himself in front of the jury. Wilton will have no option but to acquit. Especially if I refuse to move for mistrial."

"Right, you don't want a mistrial," Julianne said, "they'll just wait until the witness is recovered, if he does, and retry Tony or put together a whole new case coming at him at a different angle,"

"Righhtt," Joe said raising his brow with a smile. Generally not advisable to let the Commonwealth have a dry run at a defendant.

"No I think the second option is the most viable at this point," Joe continued. "If his condition improves Wilton may give me a shot at him before he testifies in front of the jury even though he's already denied that for now. Any comments?"

With no other discussion forthcoming, the brief meeting ended.

Back in Court

The art of legal diplomacy between Joe and Carolyn had deteriorated to the use of the telex machine. No telephone calls were made during the remainder of Monday or on Tuesday morning nor had Carolyn spoke with Joe after they had met with the judge in his chambers just moments ago.

Motions had been filed that morning.

"I understand you would like to be heard," Judge Wilton said to Carolyn.

Joe brought himself to attention preparing for Carolyn's presentation. He had requested to be heard in chambers fearing that in the open court Carolyn would take advantage of the public forum and launch into an emotional dissertation of the attack at the hotel appealing to the sensational aspect of the case. He fully expected her to run the complete gambit from the horrors of the death of the officer and the crippling of the other, to the guilt of the evil defendant.

"Request denied," Wilton ordered in response to Joe's request. "The public has a right to see the system in action. The jury won't be present and I'll give a strong instruction at the end of the day."

Joe knew that the judge was giving Carolyn a loaded gun, perhaps to compensate for the hardships in her case. With the courtroom filled with spectators and news people, he knew well whatever was said in open court would be splashed all over the news media. Some jurors would disregard the order not to watch television because they believed they were intelligent enough not to allow such input to interfere with their judgment. Others would surrender to the urge to watch themselves on camera. Still others would talk to their wives, their husbands, girlfriends or boyfriends. All would pick up opinions, prejudices, and even demands that they do the right thing and not listen to the slick defense attorney.

"If I may your honor," Carolyn started in open court. "I have submitted my motion and memorandum in opposition to the defendant's motion which asks that you limit the testimony of the confidential informant and the inmate informant to the point that they are prevented from taking the stand. I will not belabor the Court with a redundant recitation of that which is contained in my documents, but I would like to further outline the Commonwealth's position with respect to the defendant's latest attack on the Commonwealth's case."

On this breath, Joe made sure that Carolyn and the gallery noticed his 'trial' shift of weight and his obvious grimace of distaste but he bided his time having planned not to voice an objection until the choice moment.

"As your honor is aware Sunday evening last, tragically, Officer Theodore Mitchell was killed during an attempt on the life of the Commonwealth's key witness; I should say an unsuccessful attack on the Commonwealth's key witness."

Carolyn moved closer to the defendant's table. "That same attempt took from the Boston Police Department the other officer that was assigned the duty of protecting the confidential informant. Fortunately, the confidential informant was not hurt."

Joe reacted as if this were a cue to action. Jumping up he said: "Now respectfully your honor, I pray your judgment. My sister is plying to the sympathies of the gallery. We all know the second officer is alive, but, now, for the benefit of today's news, he is dead. I renew my request that these matters be heard in chambers."

Carolyn, angered by the interruption and refusing to be intimidated into silence, turned to Joe and said, "I didn't mean to imply that the second officer was dead Mr. Balliro."

Any time opposing counsel directed comment to him, Joe took full advantage before the Court had time to intervene. "Well, I apologize, Carolyn if I IMPLIED that you are auditioning for the evening news." Laughter broke out in the gallery.

Judge Wilton took control. "Okay counselors, that's enough. Miss Cheline you will attempt to be as accurate as possible and will understand that I am not one that is persuaded by sympathy. Mr. Balliro, request denied. Continue please."

"As I was saying before I was interrupted," Joe again shifted and sighed. "This matter comes to your attention as a result of the defendant's request that the Commonwealth be prevented from presenting the confidential informant, still alive, still competent, and still willing to testify despite the defendant's effort,..."

"Oh, I object most strenuously your honor," Joe erupted. "I simply cannot sit here and allow my sister to make such abominable innuendo against my client without standing on his behalf. There is absolutely no basis for my sister's classic use of accusations that are incapable of being proven. If she chooses to point the finger, then I point it back and say show me the evidence!!!"

The sheer power of Joe's challenge brought the gallery alive. Carolyn failed to respond in time to cut off the Judge's now irritated impatience order, "I WILL have order in this court or I WILL instruct the officers to clear this room of all spectators." This threat brought relative silence from those whose job depended on being present. "Now, I will not stand for another outburst from either of you or from the gallery. Mr. Balliro, objection overruled. Sit down. Miss Cheline, I advise you in the strongest terms to inform this court of the basis for your assertion that this defendant is responsible for what you have labeled a 'hit' on your key witness."

Of course, Carolyn didn't quite say that the defendant had put a hit on the C.I. but as is customary in times of court room crisis, the Judge cut through the chase and got right to the point. Fortunate or not, he had solidified the most sensational issue of the day. All New England now knew that the Commonwealth intended to accuse Tony of trying to kill the C.I. and that the prosecution had a witness who would testify it was the defendant.

With the wind out of her sails, Carolyn had no choice but to acquiesce to Judge Wilton's direct order or suffer immediate reprimand.

"As your honor is aware I have an inmate at the Charles Street Jail who will testify that he heard the defendant order his own family member to make sure that the C.I. was killed," Carolyn said quietly and defiantly.

Joe slowly stood intending to be deliberate in his movement. "Again, and with the most respect your Honor, I must object. Now we have the defendant's family involved. I must ask. Is no one spared unjustified accusations by the Commonwealth?"

Carolyn, much calmer now, waited for an answer from the bench. When none was forthcoming, she offered an explanation that distanced her from the allegations. "As your Honor is also aware this information comes to me from officers that have spoken to this man. My understanding is that this inmate overheard a conversation between the defendant and his aunt before the attack at the hotel. He was seated in the visiting area, as was the defendant, and there was little to keep him from being overheard."

"Do you have a report or statement from this inmate, counselor?" Judge Wilton asked.

"Not at this time. I had expected something by the end of yesterday and have been assured there will be a preliminary report on my desk sometime today."

"Well counselor, what you have given me is more of how things were overheard with little substance about what was said. Accordingly, I have no way of knowing whether the alleged conversation has any bearing on this case. I have to confess that at this stage the admissibility of this inmate informant's testimony is borderline at best. I am not inclined to allow him to testify."

"If I may your Honor," Joe said rising from defense table. "The substance of what this inmate says he overheard has little bearing on the admissibility of the testimony. Whether he says that he heard the defendant say 'kill him' or 'take care of him' or 'I wish he'd go away', it is clear that the Commonwealth wishes to improperly use this person to impugn the integrity of the trial, to sway the jury with intrigue, and to further prejudice the defendant. I would submit there is no basis for the admission of this testimony whatever the substance."

"Your honor his testimony falls clearly into the doctrine of consciousness of guilt," Carolyn responded. "By ordering the killing of the C.I. the defendant has admitted that he's guilty of the offense to which the C.I. would testify; the murder of Tommy Francone."

Judge Wilton, shaking his head, answered Carolyn as if he anticipated her offer. "Well, counselor, it seems to me that you've got your basis for admission confused. To a certain extent, I agree with Mr. Balliro that what he overheard has little impact on the admission of the testimony. Of course, if there was a solid basis for its admission the question would be whether what he heard has any probative value to the charge. Yet an inmate overhearing a defendant order an attack on a key witness whose identity you have had this Court's assistance in keeping concealed is a far cry from a defendant's fugitive status or flight from prosecution, which is evidence of consciousness of guilt. Also, you don't have the person that set the trap that killed the officer, injured the other, and put your C.I. in the hospital. You don't have that link and as far as I'm concerned you don't have enough. I am not going to allow error to infect this trial."

"Now if you want, you can bring other charges against the defendant if you believe you have a case, but I'm not going to allow you to bring additional charges into this case. I'm not going to allow you to put the inmate informant on the stand. It's not probative and is highly prejudicial."

In hindsight, it appeared that having the arguments held in the open court had helped direct the presentation away from the question of the C.I.'s competency and over to the inmate informant. There was more flash for the Commonwealth in the inmate rat and Carolyn's early comments blaming Tony for the hit and a few well-placed objections had resulted in the court addressing that issue first almost as if Joe had been asked his preference.

"Note my objection to your ruling," Carolyn said.

"So noted," Judge Wilton said again with a nod.

In the interest of keeping the pressure up, Joe addressed the court. "Your Honor I move that you compel the Commonwealth to reveal the name of the inmate and to deliver to the defense any and all statements or reports of the alleged conversation he overheard."

Carolyn immediately objected. "There is absolutely no basis for that request your Honor. You have ruled his testimony is inadmissible and therefore Mr. Balliro has no right to any of that material. Furthermore, I'm not going to reveal his name and put his life in jeopardy."

"Now the inmate's life is in jeopardy," Joe responded in disbelief inciting a short burst of laughter from the gallery. "The Commonwealth is seeing ghosts under the bed, in the closet, and their names are Tony Domainio. If the Commonwealth has some justifiable fear that the inmate's life is in jeopardy they can simply move him to another location. But I have a right to interview this man."

"I object again, your Honor and ask for a court order protecting the identity of the inmate."

"I'm not going to give you that protective order Miss Cheline and I'm not going to order you to either reveal the name of the inmate or turn over any material at this time. I am ordering you to deliver his name and all reports and statements to me "in camera". I will review the material in my chambers and make a decision at that time whether you, Mr. Balliro, are entitled to any of it. But be advised, Miss Cheline, if you intend to use any of the information given you by the informant directly or indirectly at this trial, you are to notify me before its use and I will order full disclosure to the defendant."

"Understood, your Honor."

"With respect to the inmate informant, the defendant's motion to preclude any information and the testimony of said informant is granted," Judge Wilton said with formality, his clerk busy scribbling authorization in the margin of the original document Joe had filed. "Now with respect to your request that we voir dire the C.I., Mr. Balliro, do you have anything to add?"

"Yes, your Honor, with the court's permission. I, as well, do not want to belabor that which is contained in my memorandum submitted this morning. But I do wish to point out some inconsistent and contradictory aspects of the Commonwealth's position."

"There is a real need for the court to determine whether the Commonwealth's witness is capable of relating whatever he is supposed to relate. On the one hand, we have the Commonwealth insisting that the defense be kept in the dark about his identity, on the other hand we have them saying that the defendant had something to do with this alleged attack on the C.I.'s life. On the one hand we have one officer dead and the other officer damaged so severely that he will not recover fully, on the other hand we have the Commonwealth saying the C.I. is fine. On this basis alone the court can recognize the need to determine if he is competent."

"Moreover the position that the defendant ought not to get a preview of the witness's testimony before trial reflects a basic misunderstanding of the purpose of the voir dire. There would be no basis for delving into trial testimony. The voir dire could be short. By this method, the court would not only be assured that this witness has the ability to testify but also that the Commonwealth can produce him. Therefore, under all the circumstances I'd submit that it is incumbent of the court to grant the defendant's motion."

"Miss Cheline, I take it you would like to be heard?"

"Yes your Honor. There is a continuing need to keep the identity of the C.I. from the defendant. Although our information is that the defendant ordered the hit, we still assert that his security would be maintained by non-disclosure. To reveal his identity to the world could result in another attempt on his life by those loyal to Mr. Domainio."

Although they were back to the octopus theory; the defendant's tentacles reaching out to control the whole world, consistent with his planned strategy, Joe refrained from objecting.

Carolyn further argued much as she had in the past against disclosure, but included in her dissertation an offer to put the C.I.'s doctor at the Court's disposal should the Judge want assurance the witness could testify.

"Do you have anything else Mr. Balliro?"

"Nothing you Honor."

"Well as far as I can see, unless Mr. Balliro can give me something more in support of his contention that the C.I. has been incapacitated and in the face of the doctor's affidavit and the assertions by counsel for the Commonwealth, I am disinclined to conduct a voir dire. I will, however, entertain a renewed motion for voir dire prior to the C.I. taking the stand if the defendant so wishes."

Joe did have more to offer. Specifically he had information from the intensive care nurse that the C.I. was hurt much worse than Carolyn let on, but he chose not to reveal it. He had been given tactical advantage both because he possessed that information and because of the ruling of the judge. Minimally he could count on a stinging cross. Maximally, he could hope for a complete breakdown of the Commonwealth's case.

"I have nothing else at this time. But please note my objection."

"So noted Mr. Balliro. Now can we get back to the trial?' Judge Wilton asked rhetorically. Turning to the court officer he said: "Trevor, please bring the jury down." Turning to counsel, he said: "Counsel - side bar."

Unknown to Joe and Carolyn, Judge Wilton had a judge's conference scheduled for that afternoon. With half the day gone he had decided to release the jury and start fresh the next morning.

A Meeting for Lunch

"Hi Pa," Joe greeted after having given his last sound-bite to the hungry media.

Jim, retired now, spent his days watching his son's trials. He had become an indispensable part of the trial process.

"Hi," Jim responded jostled out of his memories.

"Not too exciting today. We won't get to openings until tomorrow."

"Ya, I saw that."

"You want to get some lunch?"

"Sure."

Neither Jim or Joe spoke in the elevator to the first floor both aware of the unspoken rule that no conversation takes place within the confines of that crowded box; too many unknown ears. Once outside of the courthouse they instinctively headed for the Parker House on Tremont Street. "What do you think about the jury?" Joe asked.

"I wonder about that Irish lookin' guy in seat 10," Jim said. "He doesn't look too happy. He looks like he's in a hurry. He looks familiar. Does he look familiar to you?"

"I've got the juror chart in my briefcase. We'll take a look over lunch."

Once seated at the Parker House, Joe looked for the juror chart but it had gone the way of most of the file, into the havoc of his briefcase. Despite a search in earnest, Joe couldn't find it. Joe pictured him in his mind. "What was he doin' Pa?"

"He seemed impatient - moving around a lot back and forth in his seat. He kept sighin' like he was frustrated."

"I think I remember the guy you mean. William Laninan, I think his name was. I was a little suspicious of him, but I didn't think that it was too important. He looked like an average juror. You don't like him Pa, do you?"

"No."

"Well, you've been right before. I'll have Joe G. do a run down on him, see what comes up. Thanks."

"Sure," Jim said happy to be of help.

The slight lilt in Jim's response signaled to Joe that he had done something important for his father, not gratuitous by any means, which made it so much more meaningful, but important. A father and a mother spend their lives trying to make their children feel worthy.

It was such a simple gift to give that feeling back; such great fortune to be in place to do so, and such a pleasure to have it silently and mutually acknowledged.

They finished lunch amidst talk about the family and over a background of television news casts of that day's developments in the Domainio case.

Chapter 13
A Juror Still Planning

Bill sat at the bar of Flaherty's Pub in the same fever he had developed twenty minutes earlier while listening to the twelve o'clock news. Convinced that Judge Wilton was wrong to keep the information of the "C.I." and the inmate rat and any other information from him, he sat musing over the proper course of action, another stout perched in his hands.

It was natural he take up as leader of his troupe of jurors, he thought. Destiny had rightfully bequeathed him with this status. In this case, viewing himself as the enforcer of justice reigning down with firm hand upon the terror of Tony Domainio, there had been considerable self-designation. As leader, then, it was necessary he be possessed of all information. Only then could he exercise his judgment, filtering out what was necessary for the others to know in order to obtain a fair conviction.

If at some point Bill had any guilt at his deceit to the court - his designs to become a juror so that he could vote and hopefully convince the others to vote for conviction, he had covered that shame with the facade of duty to his country and his home. It was now required that he concoct a way to divulge to the other jurors the fact that Domainio had ordered the key witness murdered.

Maybe they all watched the news, he thought. Naw, can't rely on that. . . gotta have a system to tell them what's goin' on. It's the only way to be sure.

Bill's fever turned to frustration given his inability to develop a fail-safe method. He thought of taking a newspaper to court but knew it would be taken away by the court officer. Besides, he thought, I'm not supposed to be reading the papers. He thought maybe he could leave scraps of paper around the jury room but knew the room was cleaned before they brought them back for lunch. He even thought of writing on the men's room wall but dismissed that idea as stupid.

Bill's concentration was broken by Patrick Shawnessy who took the stool next to him.

"Hi Bill."

Bill knew that Patrick didn't have any money and suspected he had followed him into Flaherty's to sleaze a beer off him. This didn't put him in a politer mood.

Patrick ignored the snarled welcome and asked: "So ya got the rest of the day off?

Teddy came back so I got nothin' to do either. Can I buy ya a beer?"

"You're gonna buy me a beer?" Bill queried. "Where'd ya get the money?"

"I got money Bill, I got money. Come on; let me buy ya a beer."

"Sure, Patrick. It ain't too often. I better take up the offer before it's gone."

Bill sat in silence when his second stout was served. He lifted his half empty glass, gulped down the remainder, and reached for the beer Patrick had just paid for. He returned to his thoughts.

"What's buggin' ya Bill?" Patrick asked. "It's the Domainio trial ain't it?"

"Look Patrick, I appreciate the beer, but I got a problem I'm tryin' to sort out. I just gotta sit here until I can figure out what to do."

"Oh ya? Maybe I can help," Patrick said shifting his weight toward Bill's bad knee.

Bill instinctively pulled his leg away in a protective gesture, turned to Patrick skeptically, and was about to make a derisive remark about his I.Q., when an idea came to him.

"You know Patrick maybe there's something you can do. You owe Domainio vig, don't you? How would you like the chance to cancel that debt?"

"You don't gotta ask Bill. I'd like to get that prick off my back. What do you want me to do?"

"Not just you. You and Teddy."

"Teddy? Ya okay. He'll go along. What've you got in mind?" he asked eagerly.

"All you got to do is talk about the Domainio trial."

"What do you mean?"

"You and Teddy. All you gotta do is talk about the case."

"Hey Bill, we're doin' that right now. How's that gonna help?"

"You're a bright bulb ya know that Patrick? We ain't talking about the right stuff and we ain't talking about it in the right place."

Patrick sat still, thinking. What seemed so obvious to Bill was elusive to him. He was unable to solve the puzzle. He submitted. "Bill, I don't get it."

Bill sighed and shook his head. Slowly, with a deliberation intended to irritate, he explained. "Teddy and you hang around the court. When ya see me with a group a people get into the elevator then you know I'm with the jury. You guys get into the same elevator and you two talk about the case so everyone can hear."

"I get it Bill," Patrick said the tone of his voice revealing his limited understanding.

"Look the judge is keepin' stuff from the jury that we should be hearing," Bill continued. "Like the fact that Domainio put the hit on the witness that was gonna take the stand and that they got a guy that will say that. Now I know that, and you know that, but the other jerks on the jury don't. They could really fuck things up if they don't vote to convict him. So I need you guys to talk about the shit ya hear on the news. I can't tell them that stuff, but if they overhear it, it ain't my fault."

"I get it," Patrick said with sudden revelation. "Ya. We can do that. It'd be fun. I know Teddy would get a kick out of it."

"Great, maybe you should move around though. You know, sometimes be outside the courthouse, sometimes follow some of them to where they'd eat lunch, anywhere that they can hear."

"No problem. I'll tell Teddy and we'll start in the morning."

"Fuckin' great!" Bill exclaimed in better spirits. "It's my turn to buy. This is gonna be perfect."

Bill and Patrick stayed at Flaherty's for another three or four hours listing off what he and Teddy would talk about. They went far beyond anything the news would pick up and decided that they should expand into stories about what Domainio had been doing for the past ten years, and who his family was. Bill was smart enough to leave out any information about the death of his father. He rightly figured that should the judge or defense attorney hear that story from a juror, he would come under suspicion.

When Bill arrived home for supper he was in a much better mood. Mary took it for the alcohol he had consumed but let it go, preferring this temperament to Bill's earlier anger. Bill ate voraciously in satisfaction of his own wisdom and intellect proud at his good fortune at being chosen by fate as a leader among men.

Chapter 14
Trial Begins

Although generally considered the least sensational part of a criminal trial, the subdued and clinical opening is the greatest threat to the defendant's freedom. When delivered correctly, it will all but convince a jury to convict without the aid of any evidence. It follows, then, that a misjudged waiver of the right to make an opening statement, even when that right is reserved until after the Commonwealth has introduced all its evidence, could cause a jury to be so biased against acquittal that any defense is received with inpatient skepticism.

It is truly ironic, then, that a decision of such great importance is not normally decided after long conference and due consideration. Whatever the decision, it is usually guided by the state of the defendant's case because in order to have something to say it is first necessary that you have a case. If you don't intend to put on witnesses, then you will have to rely on cross examination. There may be little or, strategically, nothing to say in opening. It would be improper to stand and say nothing of substance.

Without an opening, the defense attorney is relegated to rebutting the Commonwealth's advantage by attacking the validity of its evidence during trial, hoping that the jury will not decide until deliberations.

Joe had given considerable thought to his opening or lack of it. He had an alibi defense. In fact, he had notified Carolyn that he would interpose alibi as was required by the Massachusetts Rules of Criminal Procedure. His and Tony's problem was that his list of alibi witnesses probably matched the district attorney's list of targeted hoods. Each would probably be sitting where Tony was someday - soon. Joe was certain that Carolyn wasted no time acquiring their extensive criminal records. Add to this the fact that they all either knew or were employed by Tony and you had a case that would carry less weight than an anorexic.

The heart of the defense was the voice on the tape. If Joe could establish a reasonable doubt that the voice on the tape ordering the murder of Tommy Francone was not Tony, then he might have a shot at acquittal. This would necessitate placing Tony somewhere other than at the location of the detectives' surveillance.

Joe had attempted to retain an expert who would testify that the voice exemplar given by the defendant did not match the voice on the tape. Unfortunately, none of the voice analysts who had reviewed the tape had been helpful. Some said it could have been him, others that it might have been him, and still others opining unequivocally that the voices matched.

Needless to say Joe had decided not to present an opening but to reserve that right until after the Commonwealth had rested. There was enough of a question both in his case and the Commonwealth's ability to successfully bring the C.I. forward that to wait to open later became somewhat the obvious choice.

He had also made a second preliminary decision that did not require such a balancing of considerations: he would advise Tony against testifying. This decision was arrived at customarily through a type of reverse logic. A seasoned attorney does not start with the premise that the defendant will testify and then determine he should not. A seasoned attorney starts with the premise that a defendant never takes the stand and is only convinced otherwise under the most drastic of circumstances. Ultimately, the decision rests squarely on the client's shoulders.

But, what if the attorney knows the client intends to take the stand and lie? Many a defendant will so much as admit to this deceit just by virtue of the many different stories fabricated over months to explain away increasing quantities of devastating evidence. There is little chance that this perjury would be prosecuted, even if blatant, unless there was clear corroboration of its falsity through another source. There is a dilemma of ethics, however, for the attorney. As an officer of the court, the defense attorney cannot suborn perjury under any set of circumstances. If discovered to have perpetrated a fraud upon the court, the attorney could face heavy sanctions, prosecution, or disbarment. On the other hand, the attorney is sworn to represent the client to his best interests and must protect the attorney-client privilege which demands that he cannot divulge communications with his client unless authorized to do so.

The solution, given that no one can stop a defendant from taking this stand, is to request that the judge, outside the presence of the jury, ask the defendant if he is aware of his right not to take a stand and whether he is satisfied with the advice given by his lawyer. The jury is then escorted back into the room, the defendant placed on the stand, and the attorney artfully asks enough questions to allow the defendant to tell his story without getting into too much detail.

It is only by this method that the attorney and the client are most protected. The attorney protected against the subordination of perjury and a malpractice claim by the client and the client protected to some degree from his own stupidity

Joe did not anticipate that Tony would insist on testifying. He would resist any emotional desire to cry foul on the Commonwealth. At Joe's suggestion he would remain as inconspicuous as possible, his anonymity guaranteed by his right not to take the stand. As a defendant, he could not be compelled to testify. Nobody, including Carolyn, could place him on the stand against his will. He had the absolute right to sit back and let the Commonwealth attempt to prove its allegations. This was Tony's only chance. If the Commonwealth failed to put in sufficient evidence to submit the case to a jury, Judge Wilton would throw the case out and Tony would walk.

It wasn't difficult to predict both the classical and igneous underpinnings of Carolyn's opening. There were certain things said and done by every District Attorney in a first-degree murder case; it was as much as policy. She started with the customary thank you to the jury, citing their patience and attention up to this day and in the days to come: "Mr. Foreperson, Ladies and Gentlemen of the jury. I would like to start by thanking you for your patience and attention in the past days and in the days to come. I know how much of a burden it is to sit in a case like this. Your normal daily routine is disturbed and you worry about your jobs and the things that must get done. The past few days have been an additional burden because of unforeseen difficulties that had to be ironed out before we could start and I would like to apologize for that."

As anticipated she moved on to an explanation of what an opening was and interjected that she was the attorney for the Commonwealth: "The Commonwealth is composed of the people that live in Massachusetts like you. I am here on behalf of those people and I represent the well-being of that community."

After a slight pause for effect, she then launched into the reason, seemingly obvious, of why she was there: "I am here because the most precious right that any of us have, the right to life, has been denied a man named Mr.

Tommy Francone." Not Thomas, but Tommy - much more personal. "His very right to life, to grow, and to enjoy his existence was taken away. And I expect the evidence will show that precious, most sacred right was taken away by this man, Tony Domainio." As she said these words she moved closer to the defense table and emphasized the defendant with her arm outstretched and her finger extended.

The first emotionally damning part of her opening completed, and after a respectable pause for added effect, Carolyn then listed the witnesses and evidence she intended to introduce to establish Tony's guilt: "In this case," Carolyn continued, "you will have the unique opportunity to hear the very words uttered that commanded the death of Tommy Francone. You will hear those words on tape. The words of the defendant Anthony Domainio." Again she pointed towards the defense table. "You each have a set of earphones on your chairs. You will hear through those earphones Anthony Domainio, very clearly and in language that will become apparent to you, tell another man to kill the deceased. The language will not be pleasant. I expect you will find it to be foul. But I expect, as well, that you will find the command to kill another human as foul, if not more."

Joe stood at this last statement and objected quietly. Judge Wilton nodded in acknowledgment and waived off the objection telling Carolyn: "Continue counselor."

"Now along with this tape," Carolyn said, "you will have the testimony of a man that was employed by the defendant and who ran his prostitu. . ."

Joe rocketed up, half expecting, but still a little shocked at Carolyn's anticipated comment. "Objection, your Honor. May we have side bar?"

At side bar Joe explained. "Your Honor, I objected because I expect that my sister was about to claim that the defendant operated a prostitution business. If that is true, I ask that it be precluded as prior bad act."

"Miss Cheline?" Judge Wilton asked.

"That is true your Honor. But since Mr. Balliro was aware of this claim throughout this matter and did not object, I did not think it was an issue."

"Carolyn, if you had given me notice of your intent to use it as I submit, your Honor, is the spirit, if not the letter of the law, I would have made it an issue."

"Okay, counselors," Judge Wilton ordered. "Carolyn, leave it that the witness was employed by the defendant. If you really think it is so vital to your case that the witness is allowed to testify that he was running the defendant's prostitution business, we will take it up before he testifies."

"Understood your Honor, "Carolyn responded."But I do want to impress upon the Court that if it is the defendant's intention to impeach the C.I. as the actual killer, then his motive for committing the crime becomes relevant."

"I understand your basis counselor. Its logic leaves me a little skeptical as far as trial strategy, but that is up to you. Leave it out for now."

Carolyn had inadvertently reaffirmed Joe's belief that the C.I. was Charlie. They believed Charlie was the hitter. He was the one Tony had running the girls after Tommy, so it made sense to them.

Carolyn addressed the jury. "This man will take the stand and testify that the defendant Anthony Domainio ordered the death of Tommy Francone and that Tommy Francone was taken to a pier in East Boston. There he was bound and gagged and strapped at low tide to one of the posts that support that pier."

Carolyn paused once again. "Now, I know that some parts of this trial are going to be very difficult for you. I am referring to the manner of death of Tommy Francone. You will see color photographs, as the Judge explained, that are very graphic. But it is necessary that you look at them for they will corroborate what this witness and the medical examiner will tell you and establish beyond a reasonable doubt that the murder of Tommy Francone was done with deliberate premeditation and with extreme atrocity and cruelty. The witness, the medical examiner, and the photos will all tell you the same thing; that when Tommy was strapped to that post, he was shot up with a drug called speed to keep him awake, and his kneecaps were shattered with a blunt instrument. The flow of blood caused wharf rats that live in those waters to feed on him while he was alive and Tommy died from blood loss and drowning when the tide came in. He lived for a long time before he died and I expect you will find he suffered." Carolyn stopped to give the jury time to visualize the scene and to absorb her words.

The courtroom was quiet; the only sound was the rustle of movement from the Francone side of the gallery. Tommy's mother, as was customary, was encouraged not to be present during the opening.

Caught up in the heat of advocacy, Carolyn launched into an explanation of why she could not tell the jury the name of her key witness: "You won't know the name of the witness that will tell you he was order to kill the deceased because, as we normally do, we are protecting him from danger."

Joe, again in anticipation, immediately stood up and objected loudly over Carolyn's last words, but the jury heard them and the damage was done.

Bill Lonnegan was visibly annoyed at Joe's interruption. He was as irritated as Carolyn at Joe's abrasive manner. He had tried to encourage Carolyn silently with nods of agreement.

"Your Honor, I move for a mistrial based on Miss Cheline's statement that the C.I. would not be revealed to the jury because he was in danger as a key witness."

"Your Honor," Carolyn responded. "My statement was purely unintentional and was not meant to suggest that the defendant was the danger to the witness."

"That is not the point and is totally unacceptable," Joe answered. "Your Honor, Miss Cheline knew exactly what she was

154

doing. She was attempting to avoid your ruling on the inmate informant. To suggest that the jury didn't draw the conclusion that the defendant is the threat to the C.I. is ridiculous.

"That is not what I was trying to accomplish, it was just a minor slip," Carolyn answered to Joe.

"Miss Cheline," Judge Wilton said, "that was not a minor slip. I'm admonishing you not to make any more minor slips in your opening. Mr. Balliro, your motion is denied."

"Your Honor, I ask for a limiting instruction before Miss Cheline continues," Joe said.

"I object, your Honor. Your standard instructions that the opening is not evidence should be sufficient. There's no need to interrupt my opening any more than it already has."

"No, Miss Cheline," Judge Wilton ordered, "this is one of those rare occasions when an instruction is warranted."

Joe returned to his seat leaving Carolyn standing in the middle of the court awaiting the Judge's words.

Judge Wilton remained standing and faced the jury. "Ladies and gentlemen, I want to impress upon you once again that the statements and comments of either attorney in their openings are not evidence. We have not started the evidence portion of this case. You are not to consider, in any event, the statement by Miss Cheline that the confidential informant is in some kind of danger. For that matter, we are all in some kind of danger just by virtue of waking up in the morning. You are not to dwell on it or to consider that statement. You are to erase it from your mind. Miss Cheline, please continue and remember the constraints of your opening."

"Yes, your Honor, thank you," Carolyn said visibly perturbed at being publicly chastised.

The effect of such an instruction was questionable under any set of circumstance. Some hold to the position that to have a judge direct the attention of the jury to any specific aspect of the trial creates a natural reflection upon a previous brief comment. In a circumstance like this, where Joe did not intend to open, it was much more lucrative to get the instruction than not.

Joe hoped that Carolyn would commit additional error by attempting to establish that Tony was out to kill the C.I. But, for now, he would have to settle with working the room. He had gained a certain control. For the moment, the judge had taken his side. Joe shifted with satisfaction, turned and made an innocuous comment to Tony for the benefit of the jury.

Bill made note of the suggestion that the defendant was threat to the witness thinking that he may not have to risk detection at all if Carolyn had her way. He could just make comment to others at some later date.

Carolyn continued with her opening attempting to regain her momentum but Joe's objection had come so late in her presentation that she had little left to say. She shifted back into policy statements again asking the jury to do its duty and to find the defendant guilty of the murder of Tommy Francone. Not surprisingly, not once did Carolyn comment on the basic principles of criminal law that are essential and immutable in any criminal trial; the presumption that the defendant is innocent unless proven guilty, the burden of proof, reasonable doubt, and that the defendant need not do anything to prove he is innocent. She had good reason for this intentional omission; these laws never helped the prosecution. To remind the jury about them during the Commonwealth's opening was to put undo importance on them.

Sandwiching her opening with a thank-you she sat at prosecution's table next to the homicide detective.

Upon inquiry by Judge Wilton, Joe reserved the right to present his opening after the close of the Commonwealth's case, turning to the jury as he addressed the Court.

Wound up in anticipation of testimony, Judge Wilton, like every judge who had painstakingly afforded every pre-trial opportunity to both attorneys, was anxious to start testimony. It was if the latches of a great floodgate were released with only its rusted hinges holding back the rising waters.

Joe and Carolyn were those hinges. Judge Wilton was standing with foot raised to kick free the restraints of patient efficiency. With the Command, "Counselor, call your first witness!" one could swear that a great breeze blew through the ten foot high open windows nudging the court officer out the door to retrieve and escort Mrs. Francone to the witness box.

When Mrs. Francone entered the room, the attorney's, again, were at side bar.

Even the stenographer knew to expect Mrs. Francone, the wife of the victim, as the first witness. Most murder trials started with such a witness. It immediately infuses the jury with sympathy for the victim's family.

"Your Honor I'd ask for an offer of proof on this witness," Joe requested.

Judge Wilton addressed Carolyn: "Miss Cheline what is it that you hope to gain by calling the victim's wife?"

"I expect that the witness will testify that the last time she saw her husband was two days before he was discovered in East Boston. That she saw him leave his Revere home at 9:00 a.m. on March 2nd. That the next time she saw him was to identify him at the Suffolk County Morgue two days later."

It was usual practice to allow at least one member of the family to take the stand to establish without a doubt that the victim was alive but now is dead. Seemingly insignificant? Absolutely. But, there was a hidden purpose. The public needs to feel a part of their system. Permitting a member of the family to become so intimate with the trial process addressed the public policy behind open justice. No legislator would risk the loss of large blocks of constituency through support of a bill that would deprive the public of such a hallowed right.

The additional twist in Carolyn's otherwise routine pitch however, was the date of March

2nd. Carolyn was going to use Mrs. Francone to attempt to repair the time variance between when Tommy was supposed to have died, according to the tape, and the medical examiner's estimate of time of death. If so, Mrs. Francone's testimony had greater relevance and if so, Joe wanted Carolyn to admit it.

"Your Honor, this is merely a ruse in order to put a weeping widow on the stand to prejudice the defendant. I object most strenuously."

"It is not a ruse, your Honor," Carolyn responded. "The fact that the last time Mrs. Francone saw her husband was on March 2 is vital to the Commonwealth's case."

"Why?" Judge Wilton asked.

"Because we expect the evidence to show that the victim died within a 28 hour period between March 2nd and March 3rd. Therefore, the testimony is crucial to the time of death."

"This witness's testimony will do nothing to aid the Commonwealth in the time of death," Joe answered. "In fact, I will stipulate that the victim was last seen by his wife on the morning of March 2nd given it insignificant relevance and I will stipulate that he is deceased."

"Your Honor, I do not accept Mr. Balliro's stipulation. The Commonwealth has the right to present its' case as it sees fit."

"All right Miss Cheline. Mr. Balliro your objection is noted and overruled. You may proceed counselor."

Joe spoke up quickly, "Your Honor, in the alternative I would ask that the Commonwealth be precluded from getting into the victim's family and the identity of the deceased at the morgue."

"Denied Mr. Balliro," Judge Wilton ordered. Turning to Carolyn he ordered, "Miss Cheline I expect you to exercise good taste in your direct."

"Understood, your Honor."

The typical Italian wife and mother, Mrs. Francone was endearing to the jury. After having been helped up the single step to be seated in the witness box, adjustments had to be made to the microphone in order to accommodate her short but not diminutive frame.

The direct examination was short. Mrs. Francone appeared to be hardened women but under the pressure of testifying, she sought refuge in the cloth handkerchief visible as she had walked past the jury.

There was no cross-examination. Joe merely stood and smiled at the witness as he addressed the court. "I have no questions of Mrs. Francone." She smiled slightly at Joe as he began to sit down. Joe nodded in acknowledgment. The jury nodded respectfully.

With the comfort of having one witness in and out of the box, Judge Wllton broke for lunch. Standing he dismissed the jury and bade them a good meal. Once the jury had exited and without fanfare he turned to counsel and said: "45 minutes, then my chambers," and walked off the bench.

Chapter 15
Later that First Day

Alone in the courtroom, Joe searched valiantly for the material on Officer Walsh. It was as if a small tornado had crossed the top of the defense table. There wasn't even order in the disorder, just devastation. It was Joe's habit to treat his files with a certain amount of disrespect, selecting documents, using them for whatever reason, and then casting them aside without care. Normally co-counsel would take on the duty of re-organization, cringing every time Joe dipped into the file, but Joe was solo for this trial and it showed.

Before Carolyn had left Joe asked who she would be calling as her next witness. Without turning to face him Carolyn had only said she would be putting in the investigation. Officer Walsh, who had been allowed to sit with Carolyn, nodded his head in affirmation with a roll of his eyes when Joe pointed to him and mouthed the question - you?

In the quiet of the court, Joe spoke briefly with his father deciding at Jim's suggestion that they eat in to give him the opportunity to be alone with the file. As Jim was leaving, Carolyn was re-entering the courtroom. He stood aside to allow her to pass. Carolyn nodded.

"Joe, I have an additional report on the condition of the C.I. I'll be filing it with the court after lunch," she said handing him his copy.

"When do you expect to call him?"

"I don't know," Carolyn answered.

"Uh, huh," Joe murmured. Pausing for a moment, waiting for the inevitable eye contact, Joe said: "Carolyn I know you're not happy with how things are going and I'm not trying to be condescending, but don't you think you're allowing your emotions to get in the way of your professionalism?"

"I don't know how you've be treated by other D.A.'s in the office Joe and I also know this is the first time we've tried a case against each other, but this is the same way I deal with every case. I am being professional. I'm sorry if you don't like it, but I'm not going to change my ways to accommodate your idea of professionalism or to make you more comfortable."

"Okay, okay," Joe said raising his hands in surrender. "Can I at least expect that you will call the C.I. after you put in the investigation?"

"Sure but I can't promise I'll produce him before I put on the medicals."

"Fair enough."

As Carolyn left the room she passed Jim who had heard pretty much all of what had just transpired. She nodded her head again as he held the door for her exit.

Joe was reading the latest on the C.I. when Jim approached the defense table. Waiting until it appeared that Joe had finished reading a one-page document he said: "I got you a diet Coke."

"That's fine Pa," Joe said his attention still on the report of Dr. Ablow.

He reached for and opened the Coke without taking his eyes of the new report, excited by the additional discovery just handed to him by Carolyn.

The C.I. had regained consciousness that morning. Of that, Joe was already aware. But, contained in this latest report were the results of a neurological done after he woke. Because neurology was among the plethora of trivial knowledge Joe had gained over the years, he could decipher that there had been significant deterioration of the C.I.'s cognitive and communicative skills. A caveat by Dr. Ablow indicated that the C.I.'s ability to communicate could be directly related to burned vocal chords, a product of the toxic gas. The doctor also suspected that his ability to recall was not related to the fluctuation in his cognitive skills and that he expected further improvement over the next days and weeks with the need of some therapy anticipated. Should make for an interesting cross, Joe thought.

He took the sandwich in his left hand releasing the report with his right. His thoughts shifted to the medical examiner's testimony on the cause and the time of death and it suddenly occurred to him that he had attributed death to a severing of the femoral artery in the left leg; massive and rapid loss of blood. If it was true that the damage caused to the femoral artery resulted in the loss of blood that caused Tommy to die, then he was probably unconscious a lot sooner than the Commonwealth alleged. It was arguable, then, that the wharf rats did not directly or indirectly contribute to his death, unless the M.E. was going to testify that they tore the artery open after the hatchet had been applied. Equally, if Tommy had been unconscious soon after the artery had been severed, there could be an argument that he was unaware of the presence of the rats.

As he jostled this issue around in his head he was interrupted by his daughter's approach, "Hi dad. Hi grandpa," Julianne greeted.

"Hi," Joe answered. "What are you doing up here?"

"I had motions in 704. I thought I'd stop by and see if you need anything."

"As a matter of fact, I do. Let's talk in the hall." Joe turned to his father and said: "We'll be right back Pa." Jim nodded.

In the hallway Joe and Julianne stood to the side of the main entrance, the little foyer leading to the eighth floor.

"You know that Francone was found tied to the, uh, posts or pole or whatever, at the East Boston pier," Joe started.

"Yeah dad," Julianne answered. "Underneath. At low tide."

"Right. You also know that the M.E. said that he had been kneecapped, shot up with speed, and that the harbor rats had eaten him."

"Yeah," Julianne said with a grimace. "I saw the pictures."

"Well, I need you to put together a motion to stop the Commonwealth from putting in testimony about the rats."

"You want me to put together a rodent motion?" Julianne asked with a smile.

"Yep. Actually that's a good way to title it. Call it a Motion to Preclude Evidence of Rodent Consumption."

Julianne shivered in distaste. With a look of skepticism she said: "I'll work on that title. There's got to be a better way to put it."

"That's neither here nor there," Joe said with a wave of his hand. "I need you to attack the cause of death. The autopsy indicates that he died from blood loss due to damage of the femoral artery in the left leg. If so, they may have no basis for all this rat stuff, especially if he was unconscious with they fed on him. And, if he wasn't unconscious when the tide came in, which is what the report says, then they have no way of knowing how long he was unconscious. So they can't tell the court how much of the rat evidence is relevant to cause of death. If he wasn't awake, he wouldn't have known the rats were there. If he didn't know they were there, we may be able to argue it wasn't cruel and atrocious to tie him to the post. It could get rid of one theory of first-degree murder.

"Uh huh," Julianne acknowledged. "Except that cruel and atrocious goes to the mind of the defendant not the victim."

"Understood, but it is still an issue over expected cause of death and if I can get a toxicologist to testify that under those circumstances the expected consequence of the injection of speed would be to render the subject unconscious, I may be able to convince the Judge or the jury that they knew he would die in his sleep."

"In fact," Joe continued, "check out an expert on that. In any event, even without the toxicologist expert I think I can fashion an argument that they didn't plan for him to become rat food; they just wanted him to know he was going to drown. That may be enough. They've got very little that says that they wanted him to suffer from the rats."

"This will tie in well with the autopsy photos. I've objected to them on the basis of prejudice - they are gruesome - but if the rat bites are out I may be able to block them individually. Plus - no testimony of rat bites."

"Did she open with the rats?" Julianne asked.

"The Judge let it in over objection but I didn't object on the issue of cause of death, I objected because of the prejudice to the defendant. I can put it all together though when I present the motion."

"Yeah but the jury will never forget the rat opening even if the judge tells them to."

"It's better than nothing," Joe responded. "Besides it will raise a good appellate issue."

"Agreed. When do you need it dad, yesterday?" Julianne said knowing the answer before the question was asked.

"Right," Joe said.

Changing the subject Joe asked if she wanted half of a sandwich.

"No thanks dad. I'm going to take off. I'll have this on your desk in the morning. If you need anything else I'll be at the office."

"Okay, thanks," Joe said with a kiss.

Julianne left, but not before leaning over to give Jim a kiss, a hug, and a "See ya, grandpa."

Chapter 16
A Plot Begins to Unravel

Trevor was the first officer back from lunch. Spotting Jim he called out: "Jim! How are ya?" It's good to see you."

"Hi Trev," Jim answered. "It's good to see you. I saw ya the past few days but I couldn't catch your eye. How're doing?"

"Can't complain, Jim. Can't complain. How's Ann?"

"Good. Everybody's good. How's your family?"

"Good."

Trevor had worked the turnstile at Suffolk Downs for a few years while waiting to get his present position. Jim knew him from the racetrack. He had worked hard labor at the track fro years; never gamble though. He walked over to the gallery and leaned on the half-wall separating the room. "A lot different than the track. A lot quieter," he said.

"Yea. I like it. Probably because I'm getting old."

"Hey, we're both getting old Jim. But this is something you never get used to," Trevor added. "They really screwed this Francone kid over."

"Yea," Jim said without further comment.

171

"Now I got a problem with the jury."

"The jury?" Jim asked.

"Yea. Tell Joe - would ya - one of the juror's just handed me a note. I don't think any of the other jurors know it. She kind'a snuck it to me."

"What's it about?" Jim prodded.

"Don't know Haven't read it. As soon as the judge gets back I'll give it to him. Where's Joe?"

"Outside talking to my niece."

"Julianne?" Trevor asked.

"Yea. He should be right back. He's right outside in the hall."

"Well, will you fill him in when he gets back? I bet the judge'll want to talk to him."

"Okay," Jim said.

"Thanks. Good seein' you again Jim. Good luck."

"Thanks Trev. Give your family my best."

"Sure Jim. I will."

"Apparently at least one juror has overheard some conversation in the elevator about the inmate informer and the defendant," Judge Wilton said in chambers, holding up a piece of paper. "I have received this note which reads as follows:"

"Dear Judge Wilton,

I was in the elevator at lunch time with about three other jurors when two men started talking about the case. I told them that we were jurors but they said they didn't care. Before we got off the next floor I heard them say a man at jail had ordered the confidential informant killed or something about the defendant doing it. I don't remember too well what exactly he said. I was trying not to listen and I didn't want to talk about it with the others."

"I haven't decided what to do about this now or if I'm going to do anything," Judge Wilton said. "I wanted to hear from you people first."

Carolyn took the lead. "I don't think we should do anything about it. If we do, it will just be emphasized."

"In other words it is the Commonwealth's position to ignore it and to go about business as usual?"

"Yes your Honor. I don't think there is any basis for any other action."

"I have a feeling that your brother has a different position. Am I correct Mr. Balliro?"

Joe had been looking at Carolyn with a smile of incredulity. "Quite a different position your Honor," he said. "I move for a mistrial."

"A mistrial!" Carolyn exclaimed. "There's absolutely no basis for that drastic of a measure."

"Your Honor," Joe continued. "I worked very hard to impress upon the Court the necessity of keeping from the jury any mention of the so-called inmate informant, not to mention the attack on the C.I. Now I'm faced with a jury that will link the defendant to the murder of a police officer through another informant that would say my client tried to have the Commonwealth's key witness killed so they couldn't hear his testimony. I'm not saying the Commonwealth had anything to do with this but something is rotten here. I don't think there is any question that the disclosure of this information, no matter how it came about, has tainted the jury and this Court must order a mistrial."

"I'm not going to order a mistrial at this late date based upon what appears to be a very limited disclosure," Judge Wilton said.

"Then I move that you individually examine each juror that overheard the conversation," Joe said. "The note says that four were present. We have four alternates. I would ask the Court to determine who was present in the elevator and that they be stricken from the pool."

"Objection your Honor. That would leave us without alternates. If just one person gets sick and can't proceed, the Court will be forced to mistrial anyway. Besides, there is nothing to suggest that what this juror heard all the jurors heard or that it will affect their judgment."

"I have to agree with Carolyn, Joe, but I also think we should at least have a talk with the one who sent this note. We can then consider letting her go or letting all four go."

Judge Wilton called out: "Trevor, can you identify the person that handed you this note?"

"Yes Judge."

He turned to both attorneys. "How do you want to handle this?"

Joe suggested that the juror be separated from the pool as quietly as possible and interviewed by the judge without counsel. Carolyn wanted to be present. It was finally decided that Joe's suggestion was more acceptable. Outside the presence of the attorneys the juror would be unaware that they had been informed of her note. Hopefully, this sense of confidentiality would encourage full disclosure. Once the interview had been completed the court reporter would read back verbatim the questions posed and the responses made by the juror. Counsel could then state their positions.

Nancy Wilcock sat in the jury room on the eighth floor apart from the other fifteen members drinking her tea from a Styrofoam cup. Her newly acquired friend, Susan, who was as quiet and as demure as Nancy and who was present with her in the elevator sat away from her seemingly in the same quiet reflection. Nancy sipped her tea respectfully wondering if she was putting too much emphasis on what she heard, but, she reflected, the Judge had ordered that they were to inform him if they heard anything about the case. Susan and the other women in the elevator appeared to be deliberately avoiding the subject but that wouldn't excuse her secrecy. Nancy knew they were doing exactly what she was - thinking about what they heard - exactly what they weren't supposed to be doing. It was impossible not to. Maybe nothing would come of it, she thought. Maybe the court officer just threw the note away.

Trevor came into the jury room and with a surreptitious glance at Nancy announced that because of the failure of the air conditioner the Judge would permit them to leave their suits or wraps in the court officers' lockers for safekeeping while they were in court if they so wished. Nancy, after a look among the others, stood and removed her suit top and followed the others behind Trevor. Once in the hallway Trevor allowed the others to pass him by, separating Nancy as she approached explaining that there was more room in the office.

"I had to give your note to the Judge," Trevor explained. "It's my job," he said apologetically. "I read it before. The Judge wants to speak to you." Trevor felt Nancy tense. "You're not in any trouble. He just wants to ask you some questions. Don't worry. He's really a very nice person and he likes people that are honest with him."

"What about the others?" Nancy asked.

"If he wants to know about them he'll ask you. Just answer his questions as honestly as you can."

"I didn't mean to start any trouble."

"Try not to worry. He's really a nice man," Trevor assured her.

Within two minutes Nancy found herself seated across from Judge Wilton in his chambers, the court reporter seated next to her, and, thankfully, Trevor standing behind.

"Mrs. Wilcock," Judge Wilton started. "Let me say right up front that I am always struck by my good fortune at having selected as jurors individuals such as you. It took great courage to notify Trevor of the incident in the elevator. You could have merely gone on without saying a word as anyone else most probable would have. I appreciate your honesty and your willingness to abide by my instructions. That being said let me say further that you are not here because I am angered at you. I want you to understand that I have absolutely no animosity for you because of what has happened. There will be absolutely no repercussions against you. Do you understand?"

Nancy relaxed a little. "Yes, your Honor."

"As I understand it you were one of three jurors in this case that were present in an elevator just about one hour ago and you overheard two rather persistent men speak about this case and the defendant. Is that right?"

"Yes, your Honor."

"Mrs. Wilcock, I need you to tell me everything you can about that elevator ride."

"I don't know, I mean, it was all very upsetting," Nancy started. "They were very rude and would not stop talking. They were looking right at me after I told them that we were jurors. They were mocking all of us. They didn't care. They just kept talking about the case. We finally got off on the second floor and walked down to the exit and there they were, waiting for us."

"Would you say that they were trying to get you to listen to them?"

"Oh - I don't know," Nancy said introspectively. "Maybe they were just mad because I asked them not to talk while we were around. Like maybe they were trying to get revenge on me or us for me saying that."

"What exactly was it that you heard? And I mean you, not what you think others might have heard."

"Well, we were all very close together so what I heard was probably what they heard, but I was trying not to listen. I mean, I was talking to the others over what the men were saying."

"I understand. But what do you remember the men saying?"

Nancy thought for a few seconds, reconstructing what happened before continuing. "We had just got on the elevator and the doors closed. I asked Susan where we should go for lunch. Before she answered, one man said something about the defendant being a punk and a wise guy. The other man said something like he was just sitting there like a wise, uh, ass your Honor," she said humbly. "I told them there were jurors in there and could they please stop talking about the defendant. The one man looked at me mad and told me that if I didn't like the conversation I could leave. They then said they hoped he would be found guilty and that - something like he had tried to get the key witness and they hoped he would be found guilty of that too because he deserved it and that they hoped the guy that heard the defendant say something about a key witness, or something like that, would take the stand. And they said that you were a, ahhh, real jerk your Honor," she said sheepishly. "That's about all I can remember. We got off on the second floor."

"I've been called a lot worse, Mrs. Wilcock. Is that all you remember being said?"

"Yes your Honor."

"Okay Mrs. Wilcock. Now I want you to think carefully. Do you think you will be able to disregard what you heard, strike it from your mind, and make a decision in this case based solely on the evidence you hear in court?"

"Yes your Honor. That won't be a problem. I didn't like those men and I wouldn't believe a thing they said."

"Thank you very much. Please do me a favor and write down for me the names of the other jurors that were in the elevator when this occurred, please." Judge Wilton handed Nancy a pen and piece of steno paper.

After Nancy finished she passed the paper to the Judge and looked at Trevor.

"Okay Mrs. Wilcock. I am going to ask that you go along with Trevor and sit where he directs you. I'm afraid this is going to take a few more minutes. Trevor, please clear the courtroom and have Mrs. Wilcock sit in the gallery and then come back. Thank you again Mrs. Wilcock for your honesty. Please follow Trevor."

When Trevor returned to chambers Judge Wilton directed him to separate the jurors whose names were on the list and to bring each one down to the back hallway near the stairs. He then explained to the court reporter that he was going to call in the attorneys and have her read verbatim the conversation he had had with Mrs. Wilcock.

Joe and Carolyn listened patiently to the monotone readback of Mrs. Wilcock's story. Judge Wilton looked at Joe in expectation.

"Your Honor, based on what transpired in chambers I renew my motion for a mistrial," Joe began after a moment of silence. "Although I recognize Mrs. Wilcock will attempt to separate what she has heard from her consideration of the evidence, I don't think we can realistically expect it not to have a substantial impact on her decision. Additionally, we have no way of knowing what the others in the elevator heard or if they have told any other jurors what happened."

Carolyn started to respond when Judge Wilton stopped her with a raised finger, "I understand your concern Mr. Balliro. It is true that I didn't ask Mrs. Wilcock if she had spoken to any others, but I think it is safe to assume, especially since she passed the note to Trevor secretly, that she has not. I am denying your motion."

"In the alternative, your Honor, I ask that you strike the four jurors exposed to those men and sequester the remaining twelve."

"I object your Honor," Carolyn said. "There is absolutely no basis for that action. Besides it would seriously jeopardize the pool should one member be unable to continue."

"I am not going to spend the next two days interviewing each of the remaining three jurors and give both of you the opportunity to take a position that I believe I can safely say will be the same as voiced here already. The delay would be onerous to this Court and to the remaining jurors. I am going to strike the four jurors exposed to these statements. I am not going to interview them or the remaining pool to determine if any others have been exposed. I am denying your motion to sequester Mr. Balliro. However, given that the exposure seems limited to the courthouse, I will swear in the court officers and have them escort the pool during the day and until such time as they are safely away from the court house and the immediate area."

"Note my objection," both counsel said.

Judge Wilton ordered Trevor to diplomatically dismiss the three jurors on the list and Mrs. Wilcock and to assure those dismissed that they were not being punished; their release was a necessity, nothing more. Once that task was completed, the jury was brought in.

As Bill sat down he became immediately and anxiously aware of the empty seats.

As the Judge explained the empty chairs of their co-juror's, directing them in explicit terms not to dwell on their absence or the reasons therefore but to pay attention to the trial and evidence, Bill's anxiety swelled to a controlled panic. It had to be Patrick and Teddy he thought. Jesus, maybe they were caught. Maybe they were ratting him out right now. If they discovered that he purposely went against the Judge's orders, the result would be far worse than the beating he used to get from his father for fighting at South Boston High School. He'd been in jail before and he didn't like it. He didn't belong there. Taking a moment to calm his racing mind, Bill figured that if they knew, he would not be there listening to the Judge, so he was safe for now. He made up his mind to speak to Patrick and Teddy, if the fools hadn't been tagged, and tell them to be more careful. But, that would have to wait because the Judge just had the court officers stand and swear they would keep the jurors away from any outside influences until they had left the area.

Unfortunately, Bill did not have that opportunity to speak to his cohorts that evening or before the next day. Too bad - if he had, the 'hammer', as his father was fond of saying, would not have come down. At least not as hard as it did. He might have been spared jail and a beating.

The remainder of the day was exhausted with the testimony of various police officers involved in the investigation of the death of Tommy, some having very little to do with the case, others merely repeating the testimony of others.

Officer Walsh, however, was called in order to admit the disputed tape and transcript of the wiretap. Joe asked for side bar. "Your Honor, while I expect Officer Walsh will be able to authenticate the tape itself he does not have the expertise to authenticate the voice on the tape. I submit that it would be most proper to determine the validity of what is alleged to be the defendant's voice before we simply expose the jury to it. It certainly makes more sense procedurally."

"Do you have an expert of voice analysis Miss Cheline?" Judge Wilton asked.

"Yes I do your Honor. I will not be offering nor requesting that the tape be played before he authenticates the voice of the defendant. As an offer of proof, Officer Walsh will simply testify to the defendant's presence at the location of the recording."

"Well your Honor, then it seems even more sensible to voir dire the expert. I myself have an expert I will offer immediately thereafter giving the Court the opportunity to rule on the admissibility of the recording. To allow Walsh to testify that the defendant was at the location before your ruling would permit the jury to draw an inference adverse to the defendant whether or not ultimately proper."

"Mr. Balliro, I take it your expert will say that it might not be the defendants' voice, right?"

"Yes your Honor."

"Well then, it really is a question of weight not admissibility isn't it? No, I'm going to allow Officer Walsh to testify about the tape and the expert to testify as to its authenticity. I will then rule on its admissibility," Judge Wilton ordered. Turning to Joe he explained, "Mr. Balliro, I'm not going to get into a battle of experts at this time. The jury can determine whose opinion to believe. Let's get on with it."

Having exhausted all attempts to whittle down Walsh's testimony, it became even more critical that a tight rein be held on Carolyn during direct examination. Most assuredly she would have designed her questioning - pro forma - to illicit a translation of each line of the text seeking, blatantly, to substitute phrases like 'take care of him' with 'kill him' or 'make it a special' with 'tie him to the post and chop off his knees'. Generally, an officer such as Walsh would be permitted to testify about street language given his common experience in the nuances of street code; a golden opportunity for Carolyn to argue the meaning of evidence through the testimony of a witness.

The substance of the tape would be only one part of Walsh's testimony that warranted serious attention. There was also his martyrdom as the sacrificial lamb on time of death.

Walsh would testify to an additional surveillance of Tony and the C.I. on March 2nd. Probably sometime in the late morning - early afternoon. It was here, he would say, at this second unrecorded and heretofore unmentioned meeting, that Tony reaffirmed his order to kill Tommy. A critical piece of evidence sandwiched neatly between Mrs. Francone's previous testimony about when she last saw her husband; 9:00 a.m. on March 2nd, and the expected testimony of the medical examiner that he succumbed to his injuries at approximately 2:00 a.m. on March 3rd. The foundation would be laid for argument to the jury that it was at this meeting that further plans were made to kill Tommy early in the morning of the March 3rd not on the 2nd as the tape seemed to indicate.

Gathering her papers for direct examination, Carolyn left the prosecutor's table, approached the podium as it stood at the furthest end of the jury box microphone mounted at its front edge, and with deep breath announced her next witness. Conspicuously, she had left Officer Walsh seated at the table, poised to stand when his named was called.

Walsh had taken great pains during side bar conference to organize the desk, re-filing papers used or no longer relevant back into the banker's box situated against the front of the clerk's bench. He had taken the cardboard box that hold the bloodied clothes of Tommy Francone, the ropes used to tie him, and the numerous plastic bags of evidentiary minutia, collected and marked, placed it in front of his legs towards the jury box and had shifted and sorted the more interesting of the items back and forth more in an effort to draw the jury's attention than to aid in its selection and production during his testimony. When Carolyn had returned to the table after side bar, Walsh, with exaggerated movement, nodded willingly his eagerness to take the stand and again leafed through the papers he had compiled for reference if needed. He again looked up at Carolyn and said, in a voice loud enough to be heard, "Yep, I'm all set. Let's go."

Of course, among the motions Joe had filed before trial was the standard motion to prevent law enforcement officials from sitting with Carolyn at the prosecutor's table throughout the trial. The Commonwealth of Massachusetts had the dubious distinction of being the only state in the nation that permitted the arresting officer or the police investigator assigned to the case to sit with the prosecutor during trial. It was not uncommon to see that investigator handling the evidence, speaking in hushed tones to the prosecutor, writing feverishly during cross examination, and generally doing all that a support staff might do, including signaling other officers to run errands of necessity or of show. It also was not uncommon for the Commonwealth to call that same officer to the stand several times to present testimony that is timely or advantageous.

Current trend, discouraged and condemned by the Federal Court, was to continue this practice. The motion had been denied.

Once at the podium Carolyn had taken time to check the order of her documents, her yellow legal pad set aside in due deference to its importance. The jury shifted its vision much like a crowd watching a riveting tennis match, to and fro, from Carolyn to detective Walsh from detective Walsh to his box of rope and bloodied clothes and from that box back to Carolyn and her papers waiting anxiously for some tense court room drama.

Walsh shifted his weight toward Carolyn as she stood looking at the Judge.

Judge Wilton allowed the annoying silence to continue refusing to acknowledge Carolyn's attention, instead looking at her directly with not so much as a nod. He chuckled to himself at her mounting discomfort but only waited, desiring to see how she would extricate herself from her own pomp and circumstance.

Bill lowered his head in one hand thinking that nobody knew what the fuck they were doing.

Carolyn cleared her throat in an effort to ensure her voice had command and asked in a much weaker resonance than intended: "Your Honor?"

The dense silence broken, Judge Wilton shifted his weight. "Yes counselor, call your next witness."

It seemed as though the whole building sighed in a muttered non sequitur. "The Commonwealth calls Officer Patrick Walsh of the Homicide Division of the Office of the District Attorney."

Walsh stood, pushed his chair free, lifted his papers and placed them under his arm, raised his right arm without stepping from counsel's table, and in doing so presented himself to be sworn affirming his allegiance to justice in a strong, deep, sincere, and loud, "I do." He turned to Trevor waiting for escort and when directed, marched to the witness box in confidence taking his seat and spreading his papers in front of him on the small ledge provided.

Once Walsh had settled in, Carolyn started her questioning with name, address, training, and experience. These familiar remembrances brought back to full force the purpose of this gathering and the trial was once again underway, the aberration of the past few minutes forgotten.

Not too soon thereafter, Joe was perched to intercede when Carolyn approached anticipated and disputed testimony.

Approaching Walsh, Carolyn handed him a document. "Now officer showing you what has been marked as Commonwealth's exhibit "A" for identification can you identify it please?

"May his answer be limited to a physical description?"

"So ordered."

"It's a tape and transcript of that tape made by myself and a surveillance crew."

"When was it that this tape recording was made?"

"May he be limited in his answer to date, day, and time your Honor?"

"So ordered."

"March 1, 1979 at approximately 9:30 a.m."

"And directing your attention to the transcript of that tape, could you tell the jury please what is meant when it is indicated that the defendant said, . . ."

"Objection." Joe jumped up before Carolyn could finish. "I would request side bar," he said with obvious distaste.

At side bar Joe lashed into Carolyn. "Your honor this is a blatant attempt by my sister to get the substance of the tape recording into evidence when you have specifically ordered that it must be authenticated before admission. I further object to my sister's leading question. The witness has not testified and cannot testify that the voice on the tape is the defendant or that the defendant said anything contained therein, as is indicated by the form of my sister's inquiry."

"I'm somewhat confused Mr. Balliro," Judge Wilton said. "I thought I ordered that she could proceed without authentication at this point?"

"Your Honor I interpreted your order as allowing her to present her witnesses out of order but this is a completely different issue.

She is deliberately attempting to have this witness testify that it is the defendant's voice on the tape. There is no reason he cannot be held to the same evidentiary constraints that he would be if the expert had testified first. That is, that there is a person's voice on the tape, not that it is the defendant's."

"I think I understand Mr. Balliro but it is really one and the same thing. However, technically you are correct. Miss Cheline, even if the expert had authenticated the voice on the tape it would still be a question for the jury. He cannot testify that it is the defendant's voice that he is interpreting. You are going too far at this time and you may not do so until such time as you put your expert on and establish a connection between a voice on the tape and the defendant."

"Your honor, if I can't have him read the transcript; I can't have him interpret it."

"That's the other basis for my objection, your Honor," Joe interjected. "There is no basis for the admission of this witness' opinion or interpretation of what was said. That's the province of the jury."

"No, Mr. Balliro, he can state what in his experience is meant to be said when things are said in a certain way. The jury can then decide what weight to put on the testimony. I'll allow him to so testify but Miss Cheline, the voice on the tape must remain unidentified during your direct unless you put on your expert first."

Carolyn had gotten lost briefly in the hyper technical grounds of the objection but was finally able to grasp Joe's objection and the Court's position

"Your Honor, may I then suspend with this witness and call my expert. I would then be asking that I be allowed to put officer Walsh back on the stand while I play the tape to the jury and while they follow along with copies of the transcript. He would then testify as to his interpretation."

"That will be allowed," Judge Wilton ordered.

"Note my objection your Honor," Joe said.

"So noted."

As Carolyn returned to the stand she realized that after all her pomp and circumstance and all of Officer Walsh's machinations before and while in the witness stand she would be dismissing him not five minutes into her direct. The affect on Walsh was notable as he collected his papers, far less collected himself, stood and stepped from the box, his hand trailing along its edge in unrequited desire. At the prosecution's table he sat like a schoolboy rebuked, his eyes roaming busily, as it might seem, over the documents he had coveted to the stand.

The affect on the jury was humorous. Joe made no outward sign at his good fortune.

The expert on voice analysis went as had been expected. Joe had had his report as part of discovery. Deftly applying classic expert cross-examination technique, Joe successfully damaged the credibility of his opinion by forcing the witness to admit that his science was far less perfect than even the science of fingerprinting and that in any event the voice on the tape could be that of any number of individuals in the community.

Carolyn offered the tape and it was admitted.

Twelve copies of the transcript of the tape, stipulated as true and accurate, were distributed to the jury to be read while they listened to the tape. But, the media, the gallery, and the Court would not be forsaken because while the jury would listen to the tape through their individual headphones, all would hear the command to kill Tommy Francone through the speakers of the intercom system.

Before the tape was played, however, Carolyn, with far less drama, re-called officer Walsh, had him repeat his name and identify himself as the same officer that had testified just one hour earlier and asked that she be allowed to stop the tape as it was played in order to give the detective the opportunity to testify about certain statements. This was permitted.

Joe asked the Court to recognize his ongoing and continuing objection to the playing of the tape and the testimony of the officer so that he would not have to jump up and down repeatedly. This was permitted.

At the close of the tape and Walsh's one-sided, self-serving but most certainly accurate interpretation, Carolyn reverently turned off the tape recorder and placed the transcript down. The whole of the jury followed suit obediently.

Much to Joe's surprise Carolyn ended her examination without giving Walsh the chance to testify about either the second meeting or to identify Tony. Unbeknownst to Joe, she had pre-planned to forgo this testimony on direct, banking on its use in rebuttal of the defendant's case on time of death or for redirect if Joe opened the door on cross hoping it then could be used to take some of the sting out of Joe's cross.

Joe slowly stood and walked around to the front of his table his eyes fixed at all times on the one inch stack of papers he held in his hand, the jury curious if he was going to bump his leg into the table's edge. He stopped with his back to the front of his desk, turned and placed his papers down, never taking his eyes up. Normally a short distance, his purposeful stride and patient handling of the documents on that same table, after they had traveled only a short six inches, made the few second journey appear to be flight across town. Officer Walsh sat watching and waiting anxiously.

Clearing his throat Joe began his examination in a small voice intending, as was customary, to gain the attention of the jury through the sheer concentration they would have to employ to hear him. Limiting his questioning to a few specific points the answers to which were unavoidable, Joe was deliberate and plodding in his initial approach. But as he asked each additional question, he would look up from his papers directly into the eyes of Walsh with less of a delay, giving the appearance that he was in much more control than some might have originally thought. The affect was that the first question came out as if it were a long pause. "You . .were . . not present . .in the room when this recording was taken, ahhh. . were you?"

Walsh unconsciously responded in suit. "Noooo."

"In fact . .you only saw the defendant enter the house some three hours earlier, . .riighhhht?"

"Yes that's right counselor but . . ."

Joe didn't let him finish.

"For all you know there could be ten rooms in that house, couldn't there?"

Walsh responded by finishing his last answer as if Joe was a child in need of patience. "There are eight sir."

"Eight. So out of the eight rooms, you don't even know which room the recording was made from, right?" Taken from Walsh's police report which indicated that the tape emanated from an unknown location inside the house, this question was designed to determine if there was a Commonwealth witness, unknown to Joe, who was present at the time of the recording.

"Yes we do know what room the tape came from," Walsh said now confident.

"You do?"

"Yes we do counselor."

"Well, you didn't know when you wrote your report on that night did you?"

"No but we found out later." Now Walsh was offering information, a sure sign he believed to be in control.

Joe's response burst Walsh's bubble of confidence. "Later when somebody told you, right?"

Realizing that he would now have to divulge the name of the other person, his self-assurance badly shaken, cursing himself for his lack of foresight into Joe's cross, Walsh shifted his eyes to Carolyn and squirmed a little in his seat.

"And that person's name is what?"

Carolyn stood to object, noting the little smile on Wilton's face. Unlike Walsh and apparently Carolyn, he knew where Joe was heading four questions earlier. At side bar, Carolyn complained that to force the witness to answer that question would be to expose the confidential informant. Judge Wilton sustained the objection but it was too late. Joe had verified what he had known all along. The confidential informant was Charlie Bottatelli.

The remainder of Joe's cross-examination focused on the interpretation given the tape recording by Officer Walsh. It was his intention to genericize the language as much as possible without re-emphasizing what was said.

As Joe came to the end of his examination, the questions came more rapidly both because the answers were unavoidable and because Walsh appeared to have lost his desire to fight.

"This recording was made on March 1, 1979 at 9:30 a.m., correct?"

"Yes."

"And according to your interpretation whatever was being ordered to happen was to occur that night, right?"

"That seems to be what was meant sir."

"Seems to be? Well that's your interpretation not mine, isn't it?"

"Yeah, that's what it looks like."

Joe turned to the bench and asked, "May I approach the witness your honor?" Judge Wilton nodded. Detouring to the Commonwealth's table, Joe pointed out to Carolyn the lines of script that would be the focus of his question. He then approached the witness chair. "Now officer would you give us again your interpretation of these lines here. Read them to yourself."

"Well, they mean that the unknown was probably supposed to do the murder that night."

"Probably officer? Probably?" Without waiting for an answer Joe hammered at the transcript with his right hand, wrist turned so as to avoid scratching the lens of his eyeglasses, "Or does it say 'TO-NIGHT, TO-NIGHT, TO-NIGHT, meaning the night of the day of this recording?"

Detective Walsh was visibly shaken. "I suppose it could be read that way," he answered resignedly.

"Just like the rest of YOUR transcript could be read any number of ways, right?"

"Objection your honor,' Carolyn said."Argumentative."

"I withdraw the question," Joe responded satisfied with the message given by the question.

"No more questions at this time," he ended.

Although Carolyn could have had Walsh testify about the second meeting, she decided not to redirect for fear that Officer Walsh would dig a bigger hole for himself on re-cross.

Judge Wilton, with sympathy, turned to the defeated Walsh and told him to step down."

Walsh did so. This time his hand did not trail the lip of the witness box.

Chapter 17
Private Investigation

Joseph Guidetti had occupied space in the Law Offices of Joseph J. Balliro for over 15 years. During those 15 years and more, employing a grinding perseverance to detail and obnoxious, but tactful, persistence, he had earned a reputation as the premier private investigator in Boston.

An unquestionable asset to the firm, as he would have been to any, "Joe G." shared with Joe a mutual respect of professional skill that was the product of decades of friendship and acknowledgement. Because of this friendship and mutual respect, because of their expertise and because they were just so damn in sync, Joe G. was indispensable to the firm proving his value over and over again in hundreds of criminal and civil cases. Diplomatic when detente was called for, threatening when force was required, he approach was based on the premise that most people were motivated by a need to demonstrate their own worth, strutting like peacocks, fanning their tails in bravado. People did not earn respect, they took it. If they could not find someone to steal it from, someone to demean to their benefit, they simply acted like they were important.

Nevertheless, it took very little to foster humility in this humanity. People were children who, when slapped, cowered apologetic for raising your ire. Joe G. had a low opinion of the human race. Hence, his bullshit detector was normally on high and directly wired into his fee.

In the alternative, naturally, if Joe G. liked you he would give you his all. He liked Joe, his family, and most of his friends. He would turn on his super sensitive bullshit detector upon request and point it where needed when retained for any case of interest to the firm. Beyond just the ability to ferret out deceit, Joe G. could ferret out a surprising amount of information on any individual. Shocking really. He could find out how many nose hairs a person had, whether it was hereditary, and what side of the family held genetic responsibility. The government held a revered place on Joe G's shit list. After all, he got all the information on his targets from information gathered by the government. Like him, they gathered all that information to hurt people not to help them. They could hurt you a lot worse than Joe G. At least he was honest. He did it for money. They did it because they could.

When Julianne had returned to the office that day, she had asked Joe G. to check out juror number 10 per order of Joe. He set to the task immediately aware from experience how crucial, sensitive and urgent was a request for any investigation concerning an ongoing trial. As a first step, he reviewed the juror chart, selection sheet, and questionnaire as well as the file and all pertinent data in order to formulate a proposed strategy for the big guy. When Joe returned from court, Joe G. had a plan for him to consider.

Joe sat in his office reviewing the rat motion Julianne had submitted per his request. It was now entitled: <u>Motion in Limine to Exclude Evidence of Injury Not Causally Related to Death</u>. He had to agree it was a much more palatable title without the mention of rodents. She had done her customary quick and efficient job. Making comment on its acceptability, he gave her the pertinent sections of the medical reports reminding her to attach them to the motion separate from the memorandum because the motion without the memorandum would travel to the appeals court if necessary.

Shifting through his mail, he asked Julianne to have Joe G. come in. She picked up the telephone and used the intercom to ask Joe G. to come into the office. Once he had arrived,

Julianne, Frank, and Steve all took seats anxious for an update on the juror issue.

"We're down to twelve jurors," Joe announced

"You're kidding," Joe G. said.

"Apparently four of the jurors were subjected to a loud conversation between two men in the elevator at lunch. They overheard them speaking about the defendant, Mr. X, and the inmate informant. Wilton dismissed them and ordered that the remaining jurors be escorted by court officers. They're using the Judge's elevator."

"You're down to twelve," Frank said. "One more and this trial goes south."

"Joe G. added, "I may have the Baker's dozen minus two. This Lonnegan guy's a real winner."

"What's up?" Joe asked.

"I read the copy of his juror's questionnaire. It's Billy Lonnegan Joe. Remember, the father. You knew him. You know this family. He lied on the questionnaire and left out that his father was shot in front of him in the North End."

"How long ago?" Julianne asked.

"Years ago. Maybe 15," Joe G. answered.

Joe smacked the palm of his hand on the table. "I knew something was familiar. I know this guy. Tony beat him up four or five times. Put him, in the hospital over money. I remember his father came to my house. Tony stuck a gun in father's face once and promised he'd get him. That was a long time ago."

"This guy stinks," he continued. "I wouldn't be surprised if he had something to do with what happened today in court. He definitely wanted to get on the jury. He wants Tony for killin' his dad."

"Unbelievable," Julianne exclaimed.

"Joe?" Joe asked Joe G. "How long would it take you to find out who his friends in the elevator are?"

"I can try and track him tonight but he's still on the jury right? He's not one of the one's that got bounced right?"

"That's right."

"Well I would think that if he had something to do with the two guys in the elevator he's probably spooked and he's going to lay low. He might not leave his house."

"You may be right but he may be so scared that he may want to talk to them and let them know what happened and to tell them to lay low," Frank countered.

Joe G. thought for a moment. "Well you may be right Frank. I can go over to South Boston and poke around but I may not have anything for you in the morning. Tomorrow I'd like to hang around the courthouse to see if I can spot these other two guys. If I can maybe I can backtrack to this guy."

"Whatever you can do Joe," Joe answered thankfully. "The Commonwealth's case is a mess. I'd like to be able to move on Lonnegan after they put their case in."

"You think they'll rest tomorrow?" Julianne asked.

"No question. All they have is the M.E. and the C.I. They'll rest tomorrow. We are working late tonight people," he announced. "I need a Motion for Directed Verdict for after they rest. One page is enough. I'll argue whatever I want to add. What is most important is that I have a motion to compel the Commonwealth to give me access to the C.I. before he takes the stand. I found out for sure who he is today and I want to put some pressure on them."

"Who is he?" Steve asked.

"Botto - Charlie Bottatelli. Never liked him much. Mean and nasty. I always figured he hated Tony the way he grumbled and complained. He was there when Tommy was killed but he didn't do it." Turning to Frank Joe asked: "Frank, what's the C.I.'s status?"

Frank had conducted an almost hourly inquest of his contact at the M.G.H. as Joe had requested. "He's awake. They've been doing all kinds of tests on him. He can barely walk but he knows who he is. He doesn't remember what happened but they are hitting him with all kinds of stimulants. The nurse says they don't really care if it's not the exact treatment he should get. They're just trying to get him ready as soon as possible. She says he's out of it most of the time."

"Okay. I want to put more pressure on them. Wilton won't stop the trial to allow me to interview him. He wants the trial over. It's turning into a circus. I want to make Carolyn as nervous as possible. In the motion, put in a request to put the doctor on first. Also, I want to address any reports they have about this guy and Tony. The C.I. isn't the one who is on the tape. They got him prepped to testify he is. He can really bury Tony if he testifies that he ordered him to kill Francone and then he did it. I want all the information I can get my hands on. The more I have for cross, the more I can mess him up." Joe paused in thought. "You know, come to think of it, they may not rest tomorrow. I may want to keep Charlie on the stand overnight. That way I get another shot at him in the morning. If they've got him pumped up it really could affect him. What would happen if he couldn't retake the stand the next day and I couldn't complete my cross? I wouldn't have had the opportunity to cross and Tony would be denied his right to confrontation. That would be a substantial issue on appeal." He took another moment of reflection. "Well, I'll have to decide that tomorrow but in the motion address the medication he's on. It gives me more reason to have the doctor on first and I may have enough to prevent the Commonwealth from putting this rat on."

"I'll give you those tonight Dad," Julianne said.

He then turned to Joe G. "Joe this whole issue of Charlie - if I hold him on the stand overnight it will give you an extra day on the juror, but I want to be able to move on him, if I can, after Carolyn rests her case. If Wilton denies my directed verdict, I want to try and kick it out on this guy Lonnegan. That may be the only way, no matter how much it pisses Carolyn off."

"How's she doing?" Frank asked.

She's bright," Joe said admittedly. "But her style is a little too bitchy. She's wrapped tighter than the varnish on a firemen's pole. Has trouble controlling herself when things don't go her way," he said cryptically. "But she's doing a commendable job under bad circumstances."

Joe G. focused back on the juror issue. "Joe, I can have a report on Lonnegan for you by tomorrow night at the latest. I may even have something at lunch break tomorrow. You want me to tie in these two guys to him if I can," he said half in question and half in request for clarity.

"If there is anything there, anything at all, I need it. I don't care if it's minuscule. It's a connection I may be able to use. Feel free to speculate Joe. You see, without a connection I'll have to go with non-disclosure on the questionnaire. It may not be enough to blow the trial. I may be able to get the Judge to ask him about his father - that sure would shake him up - but it would be better if he was hooked into some shenanigans. If Wilton doesn't mistrial then I'll have a giant issue for appeal."

"Okay," Joe G. acknowledged.

"Should be an interesting day tomorrow Dad. Mind if I hang around. I've got nothing on."

"No I don't mind at all, in fact I want you there. I may need you as a go between me and Joe G. if something breaks."

"Great," Julianne said excited about participating.

"Okay let's get to it everyone!" Joe ended the conference ushering everyone out with a word.

Joe G's closet at the office held a multitude of different outfits all generously loose at the waist to hide the .44 Magnum he carried loyally. He had never had occasion to use it, but he wouldn't hesitate for a moment if in his judgment it was necessary to pull it from its holster. He wouldn't pull it unless he intended to shoot to kill. A rule of the road. He had a family.

Joc G. chose the standard blue-collar dungarees and overhead sweatshirt. He deliberately left his day old beard, smudging some dark makeup on his hands under his nails and on the cuffs of the sleeves of his red cotton shirt. He had no expectations that he would be taken at face value. Southie was a tight community, but he figured he could get by as a heavy machinery maintenance mechanic at the MBTA construction site at the Boston end of Broadway. He didn't intend to go in too deep. Just to some of the local bars edging the perimeter. Luckily, Lonnegan lived on the Broadway end of "A" Street. He at least would have a chance at what was probably Bill's neighborhood bar.

He first called Carol and told her he would not be coming home to Dedham before going into South Boston. She wasn't too happy that Joe had to work. Their son had a hockey game that night and she had now been elected to sit and freeze during the game. Carol understood though, without explanation, and actually looked forward to an evening with her son, recognizing that her complaint was more that she would miss and would worry about her husband.

He then picked up the phone and dialed the "A" Street police station intending to ask for detective Pinardo.

"Mark," Joe hailed recognizing the voice on the private line. "I'm coming in tonight."

"What's up Joe?" Mark asked.

"Just some sleuth on Broadway and "A"."

"Got ya Joe. How long?"

"I'd say just about three hours. I should be out by 9 o'clock," Joe estimated.

"Gottcha. Thanks for callin'."

Whenever Joe could and when he had a connection, he liked to let the local police know if he was in their area. It was plain common sense. If something happened and Joe had to use his gun, he didn't want some rookie cop shooting him when they arrived at the scene. Detective First Class Mark Pinardo was a friend Joe had met 4 years earlier while investigating an insurance accident in Suffolk. The detective was the investigating officer. They had become friends mostly out of the realization that they were lone Italians in a giant pool of Irish. When Mark was transferred to South Boston he called Joe to let him know.

It was a ten-minute ride from the Harbor Towers to Southie. It probably would have been quicker if Boston hadn't seen fit to build its roads from a blueprint done by some politician's four year old child in finger painting class.

Joe pulled up in front of Riley's Pub as a first stop. He had chosen this location partly for its proximity to the corner of "A" and Broadway and partly out of irony. To this day and unexplained, there is an old photograph of Joe Balliro hanging above one of the booths near the pool table. It wasn't identified as such but there was no doubt it was a picture of Joe taken about 15 to 20 years ago.

Joe G. sat at the bar and ordered a stout. It was about six o'clock at night, after dinner, and the place was packed with locals sucking down beer and stout like there was no tomorrow. Joe looked around to see if he could spot Lonnegan. No luck. He walked over to the pool table. Figuring it would be another half hour before the next two players were done, he placed his own quarter next to the furthest from the corner pocket. Pool was always a good icebreaker and Joe had some expertise; he had a table at home. He would have no success tonight though. His leather jacket would interfere with his shot. Had to keep it on to hide the gun bulging from under his shirt. Leaving his coat on would also serve to even out the talent.

"Hey, buddy!" The bartender standing with his back to Joe had pivoted on his heels in the process of making a drink, tipped his head toward the pool table and said, "I think you're up."

Joe stood, turned, and smiled at the short, stocky, bearded man holding a pool cue.

"Oh. Ya. What's the game," he said as he approached the table.

"Eight ball," was the response. "What's your name?"

"Joe."

"You ain't from around here," the bearded man said.

"My name's Scott," another in the group said. "We play a nice friendly game here, understand'? We don't take to no sharks. Short money games. Get it?"

"Sure," Joe answered. "I just wanted to shoot a little. How's five bucks sound."

"Fine," Scott said turning Joe's hand in his. "Do us a favor. Wash your fuckin' hands, will ya. You'll get fuckin' grease all over the stick and table."

"Sure. Be right back."

Joe headed for the men's room.

Scott waited for him to leave and turned to the others seated and standing around the table. "He's got to be a pump jockey. They fuckin' eat with those hands. Do ya believe it?"

Joe returned with most of the makeup off his hands careful to leave the majority of it under his nails as if it was ground in. Returning to the table, He dispatched Scott with some calculated difficulty.

"Pure luck," he commented. "I never make that bank shot."

During the second game, the questions started coming from Scott more to bother him during play than to pry. Luckily, no one else at the bar was working the MBTA station. Joe had counted on that. City construction never used locals. It wasn't profitable.

"I got a son in Wilmington that's a lawyer," Joe answered to a question about his family. "He does personal injury work. Shit load of money in car accidents."

"Lawyers are a bunch of crooks," Scott answered. "I got in some trouble a while back and the fuckin' lawyer took two grand for nothin'. I was in court once. He wouldn't give me no money back."

"Ya, criminal work is shit," Joe said. "My kid won't go near it. But he likes to follow the big trials. Like this Domainio trial."

Joe sensed no suspicion at that comment but stopped talking long enough to take a shot anyway. "I guess he likes the blood and gore. He used to like that ghost shit when he was a kid. You must of heard about the trial."

"Oh, ya. Everybody's heard about it. Ya can't miss it. It's all over the news," Scott chimed in.

"Ya. We know a guy that's on the jury," one of the men added.

"Ya. And we know the asshole on trial," another said.

Scott took control of the conversation with an air of authority; after all, Joe was his friend first. "We hope they fry that guy. He made one of our friends a crip for life."

When Joe heard 'crip' he could feel his adrenaline flow. "Oh, yeah? Did they get into a fight or something?"

"Fight - fight - ya couldn't call it a fight. That shit-bum Domainio and a couple of his stooges mugged him. They broke his leg twice. The punks waited until he got out of the hospital and did it to him again. He's never been the same."

"Jesus," Joe exclaimed. "Broke his leg after he got out of the hospital? No shit. What did they do, wait at the front door until they released him?"

"Just about," Scott said. "He owed that punk money and when he didn't pay he was gonna keep puttin' him in the hospital until somebody paid. I guess he finally got his money."

"Jesus," Joe said quietly. "This Domainio guy ain't nice especially what he did to the guy he supposed to have killed."

"Oh, he didn't kill that guy. Not with his own hands. He had some of his stooges do it. The same guy they got that's gonna fink on him is the one who did it. That's if he's alive."

"That's the guy Domainio ordered killed in the hotel," another player added. "Greasy bunch of rats."

That comment brought a round of chuckles from everyone. Joe G. smiled to join in. "Think he'll get the chair?"

"We don't kill garbage in this state," one of the men said.

"Ya," another said. "We store it forever."

Scott chuckled. "They'll put him away for life if Bill has anything to do about it."

"Who's Bill?" Joe knew the answer.

"That's they guy who's on the jury. Fuckin' Domainio killed his dad too. Shot dead in the North End. They never went after the punk, though. Couldn't pin it on him I guess. Bill will even the score."

"He lucked out getting on the jury then."

"What comes around goes around," Scott said. "We'll all be there when the Judge puts him away for life and we'll clap."

That final comment by Scott seemed to put everyone into a somber mood. Joe G. lost the next game and ordered a round for the three men near the pool table. He returned to the bar and spent the next hour or so drinking stout and chit-chatting with the locals. He was careful to avoid bringing up the Domainio trial for fear someone would eventually get suspicious. He didn't want to make himself obvious. He wanted to return tomorrow night and hopefully spot one of the players. For now, he had enough. It had been a productive night, Joe thought, with the local smucks.

The drive back to the office was as mechanical and as forgotten as were all after a round of high-energy undercover work - much like a ten-minute brain lock in the middle of the day. Joe reviewed the information he had gained listing items repeatedly so that they would be available for his report. When he was satisfied that he would not forget even the most insignificant detail he made a mental note to phone Joe once he got to the Towers.

Business completed, Joe mulled on the uselessness of these stupid Micks, there loud mouth wives, and their wiseass kids whose sole ambitions were to grow up and be just like Tony Domainio. Ironic.

Chapter 18
The C.I.

Charlie woke slowly. As soon as his sense of sight and hearing returned panic set in. Not understanding where he was he started to sit up in his bed. The sudden shift in minimal altitude and the resultant nausea caused his stomach to turn in protest climaxing in unrelenting retching. When control returned he swallowed through a fire fueled by a rapid opening and closing of his throat as he gasped for breath.

As he lay helpless, his pain was further irritated by a high-pitched noise coming from somewhere in his head. Tears of pain, desperation, and fear dripped down his face. In a moments relief he saw that there were people all around him. One man was making sounds he couldn't understand. Charlie just looked up at him as he faded again into unconsciousness.

"Nurse increase the IV and monitor every half hour," Doctor Ablow ordered.

Cheryl Fieri had been on duty for 32 hours with a short 3-hour nap in the doctors' quarters 12 hours earlier. Doctor Ablow's orders had just cancelled her hope of getting any more rest until the patient woke and other more important personnel were needed. "Yes, doctor," she said.

Dutifully, Cheryl loosed the pressure on the IV drip gauge feeding a solution of antibacterial fighting drugs increasing the volume that ultimately entered the damaged blood vessels and tissues of Charlie's lungs and throat. Unfortunately, no medication could assist whatever healing was scheduled to occur in his mind. Cheryl decided that the doctor's orders weren't too awful. An increased IV usually meant the patient was better able to assimilate the treatment and therefore would recover at a faster rate. Checking on the half hour might get her home one half hour earlier.

Once back at the intensive care desk outside the glass enclosure housing Charlie, Cheryl took to her record keeping duties in a practiced exhibition of total concentration.

As did most trained nurses, she attempted to assure the doctors standing nearby that she was attending to her obligations and not eavesdropping on their professional banter. In this aura of confidentiality, Doctor Ablow fully disclosed the condition of Charlie as well as his opinion of the district attorney's desired course of treatment. A disclosure to be divulged to Frank in just about one half hour.

"I can't say that I fully agree with this course of action," he said to Dr. Shepard. "This attempt to bring him back to consciousness so that we can prepare him to take the stand will inevitably do more harm than good. I think that this is fairly obvious given his initial reaction."

"I agree with you to a certain extent," Dr. Shepard said. "But consciousness and his reaction were inevitable, nevertheless. The sooner we get voluntary motor skills, the sooner we can access the appropriate course of action. He did seem to respond with the fear one would expect."

"That's true but let's try to temper any radical treatment with conservative good sense. If necessary, they can postpone his appearance. If not, then they will have to face the prospect of a less than competent performance. The result may be both damage to his health and an acquittal for Domainio. My interests as his physician and the D.A.'s are intertwined but my interest in this man's health will supersede the law."

"Understood and I fully concur," Doctor Shepard responded.

Cheryl understood as well.

Charlie's dreams had become his reality, his momentary glimpse of reality a nightmare. He had existed in a world of fluid since the attack, literally swimming in his own thoughts, apart and distinct from being one with them. His selfness became so focused and defensive that he lost his ability to identify himself as the one who created the random array of confusing images. He believed that inside himself, he was watching another person's life and he was confused and paranoid at the intrusion into his mind. He had lost the balance of "Id" to the relativity of comparison. His identity became divided and incompatible and an extraordinary crisis waged in his mind. He, himself, watched himself watch another person in his mind. The separation was total. Control was recognized in those moments when the random array of images slowed to a halt and he could talk to his own image and attempt to guide it by logic. Charlie knew who he was and who he wasn't. He wasn't his own image in his mind. From that he was distinct. He wasn't the other whose images raced blindly past that image of him. He was a reporter of that information should anyone ask. His responsibility not to banish but to assist; not to void his mind of senseless imagery but to direct that imagery, protecting its existence as a parent would protect a child, and to thus give it purpose.

To Charlie, Charlie was normal. His plainly was not aware, however, of the world he had left behind in room 1411 of the Bradford Hotel.

Chapter 19
What is going on?

Trial food was taken at times that would least cause digestive havoc. Necessarily, then, it was wise not to indulge in the fancier fare of the major restaurants in Boston, but to exist on foods prepared at home with an eye towards the gentle and nutritious. An added benefit of such a practice was the atmosphere. Preparation of dinner allowed the all-consuming thought processes of trial litigation to continue in a time of relaxation and therapy, somewhat withdrawn from the anxieties of the legal profession. This was a time that Joe found to be most conducive to creativity.

For Joe it always seemed that by the time dinner was ready to be served he had developed some hypothesis that would need servicing and exploration while he ate. It did not matter how long it took to prepare dinner, he always sat down ready to embark on the next logical succession of evaluation. Armed with years of experience and an established memory of case authority, this was the time to apply a presentation to the theory, to envision what representations could or should be made to the Court in an effort to reach the desired end. The last test was one of ethics - the propriety of either the manner of reaching the desired end or the propriety of requesting the desired result.

During the time it had taken to build his dinner Joe had constructed the issue. Much like being stocked with the proper ingredients to prepare a variety of meals, he was also stocked with information that would dictate a variety of options. Joe had known throughout the trial and, indeed, ever since he first spoke to Tony, who the C.I. was. Things had radically changed with the cross-examination of Officer Walsh. He now had the opportunity to divulge his knowledge to the Court. It was much like having the key to a forbidden entrance barred by Officer Walsh. He had stepped aside. Now the question was to use the key, to turn the lock, to grasp the doorknob, to open the door, to step through, or to wait. Joe had decided to use the key. He now had to decide how far to enter.

In the morning, he would notify the Court that although he had had suspicions prior to the testimony of Walsh, he now knew who the confidential informant was. This would be done for two reasons. One, to state the obvious, and two, to attempt to remove the specter of the defendant causing some harm to the witness.

There were additional reasons. The Commonwealth was like the schoolyard bully always fully confident in its size and power. Defense strategy would necessarily involve putting that bully on the defensive. Joe would request that the Court compel Carolyn to divulge whether the witness was Charlie Bottatelli. Of course, Carolyn would balk, but Joe knew that the Court would at the very least compel her to acknowledge if he was correct.

As Joe sat at his long black marble table in the dining room of his Harbor Towers condominium taking in the much-needed sustenance he had prepared and gauging what he would do and what he would ask the Court to do with this information, the phone interrupted his thoughts.

"Joe? It's Joe G."

"Hi Joe. What's up?"

"I just wanted to report back to you on what I've discovered so far. It might be important for tomorrow morning."

"Oh. Okay."

"I went over to Riley's in Southie. Apparently, your juror lives around the block from the bar. It's the local pub for the area. I was right about Lonnegan. He's the guy you know. They never found out who killed his father but my pool buddies said they know it was Tony. Plus they said that Lonnegan knows it was Domainio. I didn't run into him but the locals said that he was going to even the score. They also said Domainio had crippled Lonnegan, broke his legs a couple of times. Once, when he got out of a hospital. Tony put the guy in the hospital and when he recovered he broke his leg again. That must be when his father paid."

"Yep, I remember." Joe asked with a scowl.

"Unbelievable. There's a whole damn conspiracy. This is incredible. You got anything that might I.D. the men in the elevator."

"No. Not yet. But I'll be at the courthouse in the morning to see if I can spot them."

"Good. Whatever you do, don't tell anyone who you are, including the court officers, if they don't know you. Don't come near me. If you need me send me a note."

"If you see them stand next to them during break. I'll know who you mean. What I need is a stronger connection between Lonnegan and these two. It's the strongest way to corroborate the prejudice I need to mistrial. See what you can do. I'll see you tomorrow."

"Okay. I'll write up a report for you and leave it on Julianne's desk. That way you'll have it for the morning."

"Great. Do up an affidavit about the investigation in case I have to use it tomorrow."

"You got it. See you tomorrow."

As Joe sat down to finish dinner, he shook his head in amazement. Although he believed that nothing should phase him after all his years in practice - he had pretty much seen it all - the way this case was unraveling was truly a lesson in human nature and the wasted energies of misdirection.

Chapter 20
Stress of a Prosecutor

Carolyn was awake at 4:30 a.m. having been unable to persuade her mind from racing with disjointed and incomplete thoughts. Interspersed among this work related menagerie was a disturbing plea that she must beat Joe Balliro and put Domainio in jail for life or she would have to face the horror of failure. She had finally kicked off her covers in disgust and was now sitting on the edge of her bed shaking her head back and forth in an effort to clear her mind.

Standing and walking out of her bedroom she glanced, as was her habit, at her side profile as she passed the large mirror of her dresser. Dressed in a negligee she could see her figure through the sheerness of the fabric. The demands of her job had completely overshadowed the demands of her physique. Although not appearing slovenly, she could see the small bulge of her stomach over her panties and the noticeable weakening of her chest muscles in the slight drooping of her breasts. Her depression deepened.

Single, with no time for a social life, she had surrendered her life to work, squelching any motivation to exercise. She had no one to keep interested and no time to seek companionship so she ignored any reflection on how she appeared to others. She returned and sat down once again on the edge of her bed, placed her head in her hands and concentrated on clearing her mind of her depression and focusing on the trial.

A long shower was in order and helped considerably in erasing the torment of self denunciation. Feeling foolish for allowing herself to indulge in self-destructive thoughts, Carolyn psyched herself up for the most important day of trial. Today she would present the medical examiner and the C.I. She would prefer to delay Charlie until tomorrow. This would give him more time to recover but she knew that Joe would be pushing for his appearance today.

It didn't matter. She was stuck with his condition, but with the support of the doctors she was confident that at least the crucial aspects of his testimony would surface. That's all she needed.

When Carolyn arrived at her office at the Suffolk courthouse, she immediately recognized a report from Detective Sullivan on her desk - late. She had demanded a report of the inmate informant two days ago. She half expected it would be late. Sullivan would do anything to make it appear that he was not strictly following her dictates. She had challenged him. He was making his male statement - marking his territory. Carolyn had dealt with this type of power struggle before and knew she would again. It was part of the politics of the job and very much a part of being a women district attorney in Suffolk County.

The supplemental report was short enough that it took no time for Carolyn's teapot to reach whistle. "...Mr. Mandrake further reports to this detective that he heard the defendant Domainio order to his aunt that the C.I. be taken care of as soon as possible as he was the person that he (Domainio) had ordered to kill the deceased Francone..." Carolyn re-read this statement once again before picking up the phone and dialing District D.

"This is Carolyn Cheline, District Attorney's Office, put Detective Sullivan on."

"Detective Sullivan is on a case and not available," the female voice responded.

"Look, he's on my case. Where is he?"

"Detective Sullivan is not in headquarters," the patrolwoman answered.

"Beep him and tell him to get up to my office stat."

"I will attempt to locate him for you."

Hanging up the phone Carolyn commented to herself at what assholes these old cops could be.

Sullivan was in the posh Back Bay section of Boston at Stephan's Cafe having his morning coffee and danish after a long night of roaming around the North End taking notes on some of his favorite lowlife. When his beeper went off he mouthed his frustration through a half chewed bite of danish. A phone call and ten minutes later he was on his way to Suffolk County courthouse knowing the reason why he wasn't on his way home to bed.

"Good morning, counselor," Sullivan greeted as he entered Carolyn's office.

Carolyn ignored his greeting. "Detective, when is it that Mandrake gave you the statement that is contained in this report?"

"Yesterday. And I wasn't alone. I was with Prost."

"And this is exactly what he said?"

"Yep. That's what I heard."

"And this is what he'll say on the stand if I call him?"

"Yep."

Carolyn put the report down on her desk purposely turning it face down, folded her hands in front of her and looked at Sullivan.

"Do you want to explain to me why it is only after the Judge ruled not to permit his testimony because it wasn't enough to show consciousness of guilt that all of a sudden you produce a statement that directly links Domainio to the hit at the Bradford?"

Sullivan ran his hand through his sparse hair. "Ya know you always look for something underhanded whenever I give you somethin' you can use. Why can't you just take it on face value? I tell ya he'll testify that way, he'll testify that way."

"Detective I want to know how this statement came about."

"I told ya. I saw him yesterday and he told me what I wrote there."

"Of course, if I check the log at the jail, it will show your visit and if I check with his lawyer he'll tell me he gave you permission to talk to his client. In other words, everything will fit neatly."

"You tell me you're gonna use him and it will," Sullivan said coyly. "Besides, he asked to see me so I had no reason to ask his lawyer."

"Where did you see him?"

"At the jail," Sullivan didn't like being grilled. "At the fuckin' jail, counselor."

"Okay, okay, detective, don't use profanity I'm warning you. I've had just about enough of your attitude. Watch your step." Carolyn picked up the phone and dialed the Charles Street Jail. Sullivan leaned back on his chair confident the story was solid.

Larry, working the desk at the jail since 11:00 p.m. yesterday picked up the phone putting Carolyn on hold while he checked the whereabouts of Mr. Mandrake the day before. "He's been in the infirmary for the past three days with a broken wrist, two black eyes, and some busted teeth. I've got no record of visits."

Carolyn put down the phone and looked at Sullivan. "You're out of luck, detective. He's been in the infirmary for the past three days. No record of visits."

Sullivan sighed raising his eyes to the ceiling. "So what. Jesus, counselor. Check the fuckin' law. I don't have to log my visit. I'm a cop. What the hell you investigatin' me for? I'm tellin' ya I saw they guy. This is what he told me. I'll take the stand and tell the jury that. Your ass will be covered."

"Get out of my office, Detective. Be happy I don't report you."

"Report me, report me!" Sullivan exploded. "For what counselor? For doin' my job? You miserable bitch!" Sullivan was standing now leaning over Carolyn's desk. "You're gonna report me? Who the fuck you think you are you piece of crap? Report me! I'm gonna make your life miserable you stupid puss. By the time I'm done with you your gonna wish you were on trial!!" Sullivan was in an Irish rage his face flushed with crimson. He made no effort to close the door when he left heading across the hall to the chief trial counselor's office. Carolyn could hear him swearing as he entered Room 817. Carolyn knew Ron Cleary would be in. Habitually he arrived at work as early as she.

Ron Cleary had been chief trial counsel for the past fifteen years. He was emotionless, straightforward, short in response and not very sweet. His descriptive index included a panoply of ethnic pejoratives notably lacking in Irish decent. He was also of the belief that there were some disturbed judges who were hell bent toward acquittal. Ron viewed such an attitude as traitorous. He had either worked with or supervised a great many now sitting judge's when they were young district attorneys. As a point of fact over 90% of the judges sitting statewide were ex-prosecutors, assistant attorneys general, or assistant United States attorneys. Having spent time battling the biased system, having spent time dealing with a constitution designed to aid the defense, having spent time day by day battling the losing war against the scum that wallows in their own filth creating more disease and dirt by hurting, killing, stealing, raping, maiming, torturing, burning, over and over, again and again, they alone should realize that the only way to put the system into equilibrium is to help the Commonwealth at every turn not to hinder them. The solution was certainly not to let a low life like Domainio off the hook.

Cleary remained always hated by defense attorney's by way of a well-deserved reputation for being very sleazy. He picked his trials carefully not only for their sensationalism but also for their winability. He had a long string of convictions none of which depended on whether the defendant was guilty or not. Tall, with straight mouth, he ruled with disdain. Any subordinates causing him aggravation usually found themselves in Pittsfield trying wild game violations. His ego was great and his trust in women attorneys non-existent.

This Sullivan was well aware.

A few minutes later the intercom ordered Carolyn with the report into Cleary's office. She inhaled deeply as she crossed the hall attempting to counteract the effects of Sullivan's tirade.

"Let me see the report, Carolyn," Ron said as she entered. Sullivan was quiet but remained angry. Ron reviewed it quickly "What's the problem?"

"He's lying Ron."

Sullivan responded immediately. "Where the hell do you get off callin' me a liar?" He turned to Ron. "You've known me for ten years, Ron; I don't have to take this shit from this flunky. I never had to take it before and I don't have to take it now."

"John, no one is saying you have to take anything," Ron said diplomatically. "Carolyn, no name calling."

Ron sat and read the report again. He turned to Sullivan and asked if he would testify that he saw Mandrake at the time and date memorialized in the report.

"Ya, I'll testify to it," Sullivan responded looking at Carolyn.

"Will this kid hold up on the stand?"

"Ya, he'll hold up as soon as I talk to him."

"Use it," Ron ordered to Carolyn.

Carolyn knew he would support Sullivan but she was determined to at least attempt to convince him otherwise. "Ron, it won't hold up. Joe Balliro will rip it to shreds."

"I don't care about Joe Balliro. He's nothing. Mandrake's in the infirmary. As far as we are concerned, Domainio put him there. Show Judge Wilton the report and ask that he be put in protective. I want the judge to know that Domainio beat Mandrake. The detective here will back you up." Ron turned to Sullivan. "Will this kid say Domainio beat him up?"

"No problem, Ron," Sullivan responded with palms up.

"Use it to force the plea, Carolyn. Your case is falling apart. Use it so Balliro will talk to Domainio about the plea."

"I took the plea off the table Ron."

"Put it back on. If he doesn't go for it come talk to me before you call Mandrake. We'll get an affidavit from the detective to support your motion. That way Balliro won't get a free shot at Mandrake. Any questions?"

"Ron, for the record I don't like it."

"There are no microphones in here Carolyn and for the record I don't care what you like. I want a conviction. You get it for me. That's it and that's all."

Ron dismissed Sullivan with a hand shake. He dismissed Carolyn with a clear message that she 'better win the trial or else'.

Once outside the office Sullivan couldn't resist gloating on his win. "All right, COUNSELOR," he said sarcastically, "you do up the motion, I'll get you a signed affidavit in my words."

Carolyn ignored his gloating. "I want it on my desk in one half an hour," she ordered.

Chapter 21
Trial and a Judge's Perspective

Judge Wilton sat down in his chambers noting with dismay three new, large motions with memorandum from counsel. This case was a monster. Sometimes it seemed that there was a conspiracy to grind the wheels of justice to a halt. Did attorneys consciously attempt to aggravate, burden, and stress the trial system? He had four cases backed up in his session - all jury trials. He had the Chief Administrative Justice calling him every other day for an update on his trial and he had the magistrate in the first session asking for a daily estimate on when his session would be free. Despite all this, he had to ensure that Tony Domainio got a fair trial. That meant he had to address with all due deference and hopefully with all due speed each of the three new, large motions with memorandum from counsel. Expecting, then, that the motions would be dealing mostly with upcoming witnesses, evidence, or, minimally, with testimony already given, Tim selected Joe's rodent motion seated on top on the pile.

The defendant's Motion to Exclude Evidence of Injuries Not Causally Related to

Death was immediately dubbed as the "rat motion". This would make for interesting conversation with his colleagues. He reviewed the attached medical records of death and decided without reading the Commonwealth's opposition, for there was none, that unless otherwise convinced, he would deny this request. Carolyn was lucky she had argued that the murder had been cruel and atrocious. The evidence of the rat bites would come in under the theory that Francone was tied to the posts, his knees shattered, shot up with speed because the defendant knew he would suffer when the rats attacked. The fact that there were rats in Boston Harbor could not realistically be disputed.

He continued to the defendant's new motion for disclosure of the C.I. and access to him for interview. He knew this would be coming. It was clear everyone now knew the identity of the confidential informant. Joe would have been remiss in not requesting access. Joe would be permitted to interview him when he was brought to the court before he took the stand in order to cut down on delay and satisfy the requirements of the Constitution.

The final motion was Carolyn's renewed motion on the inmate informant. Judge Wilton sat back on his swivel chair, exasperated, his anger building. He tempered his irritation at this now revived issue remembering only moments ago he had recognized Carolyn's persistence as a positive virtue. He noted immediately that there was an affidavit attached. He flipped to the rear of the memorandum. Detective Jonathan Sullivan - not surprising - I rule that they don't have enough, and wow, what a shock, they get enough - how resourceful. After reading the body of the memorandum, and now definitely irritated regardless, he placed the papers down and pressed the buzzer and called to Trevor. "Get both counsel in here."

Trevor exited chambers and was met with the expectant eyes of both attorneys. He took a couple of steps out of the view of Judge Wilton and mouthed the words 'he's pissed' as they approached him.

"I've read both your newest batch. Mr. Balliro, evidence of the rats will be allowed and you can interview the C.I. before he takes the stand. Carolyn you will have him available. Is there any reason you cannot now divulge his identity?"

"Yes, your Honor. Based upon all the aforementioned arguments I have set forth previously."

"Mr. Balliro?" Judge Wilton asked.

"Your Honor, we both know who the C.I. is. His name is Charlie Bottatelli, an alleged associate of the defendant. For the Commonwealth to persist that nondisclosure is necessary at this juncture is ludicrous."

"Carolyn, is this man's name Charlie Bottatelli?"

"Your Honor, I stand on my position that nondisclosure is warranted."

"Understood. I am ordering you to answer."

"Yes, your Honor, his name is Charlie Bottatelli. May I have an order that this not be divulged to the defendant?"

"Your Honor," Joe said, "the information could have come to me from only one source."

"It's out in the open now, Carolyn. I am not going to interfere with the attorney-client privilege and order Mr. Balliro to withhold information from his client." Judge Wilton then turned to Carolyn with some vigor picking up her inmate informant motion. "Moving on, Carolyn, I am more than a little upset that conveniently after I rule that this inmate may not testify based upon your proffer your position is significantly strengthened by affidavit. I am also irritated that you have suggested that the inmate has suffered a beating at the hands of the defendant. Would you care to justify this newly acquired and neatly relevant information?"

Joe knew that this was the source of the Judge's anger. He had indicated as much to Carolyn when he was handed the motion this morning. It had been the first time that he had reacted with anger.

"This is total crap, Carolyn. You've gone too far. If you want to play the Cleary game, you're going to get the Balliro defense. I am going to take great pleasure in seeing you squirm when the Judge tears into you on this and I am going to take every opportunity to make sure he does."

Carolyn hadn't responded and Joe felt some chagrin at his outburst when it immediately became apparent that she wasn't the responsible party. She had been ordered.

"Your Honor," Carolyn explained, "when I arrived at my office this morning the report you have was on my desk. I called in Detective Sullivan and proceeded to conference this matter with my supervisor. It is the position of the office of the district attorney that because an additional statement was given directly implicating the defendant and that the inmate will testify to that fact and the fact that he was attacked by the defendant gives the original offer the added indicia of trustworthiness and relevance necessary for its admission on the basis of consciousness of guilt."

"Judge, if I might say something?"

"No, Mr. Balliro, I have something to say. I am ordering Mr. Balliro immediate access to the inmate now. He will be escorted to the jail by the court officer. You will be present and I will be present. I am also ordering all records of visits to be provided when we arrive to the Court and to all counsel. We will conduct an interview of this informant before we continue today. Miss Cheline, you had better pray I do not find any discrepancy in what the records show or what this man says. Now, of course, none of this will be necessary if you withdraw your motion. Do you wish to do so?"

"Your Honor, may I contact my superior before I make that decision?"

"I will allow you that opportunity, but make it quick. Five minutes."

Recognizing that this motion was Sullivan and Cleary's doing not Carolyn's, Judge Wilton had artfully given her grounds to request that the motion be withdrawn. Otherwise he would spend a day traveling to the jail. That, he knew, was something they would want to avoid.

When Tony was apprised of his possible early return to the jail he laughed quietly. "They're gonna get their heads handed to them. That guy's not gonna say a word. They're lucky if he docsn't tell them to fuck off."

"You know Tony, this wasn't necessary. I had it handled." Joe said.

"Let's say, it has been handled," Tony smirked. "Fuck'em. Hey I'm supposed to assist in my defense, right?

Carolyn had directly left the courtroom after chambers, crossed the hall and entered Ron Cleary's office. She now returned in tow of the chief trial counsel.

Without even minor pleasantries, Ron boldly addressed Judge Wilton. "The Commonwealth has no intention of withdrawing this motion. What you propose is totally unacceptable. The Commonwealth will not be a party to it and objects strenuously to the court's interference with the presentation of its case. I demand a ruling and the opportunity to appeal your decision."

"Sit down," Judge Wilton ordered.

Ron made no attempt to obey.

"Mr. Cleary, I know who you are and you know who I am. If you do not sit down I will hold you in contempt and you will spend the day among those whom you seek to prosecute."

"You may very well hold me in contempt, but I will not be held. I am not on trial."

Judge Wilton stood the veins on his neck visible. "Mr. Cleary, if you do not sit down, I guarantee I will do everything in my power to ensure that you are on trial, that you are reported to the Board of Bar Overseers, that you do not practice during that time, and that the reasons for this action are public knowledge. Now, SIT DOWN!"

Trevor moved closer to Ron directing him to a chair with his hand. Ron's fear of political reprisal motivated him to obey. The last thing he wanted was public sympathy to shift against the Commonwealth.

"Now, you listen and you listen closely," Judge Wilton continued. "I have every reason to believe that this affidavit is fabricated. As far as the allegation that the defendant assaulted the inmate is concerned, your blatant representation of that fact can only be supported by the inmate. I will take into consideration that if he has been assaulted he may not want to state so, but I will not take this affidavit on its face. You have proposed to me a set of circumstances that in and of themselves are suspect. I will NOT allow you to infect my court or these proceedings with falsehood and innuendo. As far as your attitude is concerned, Mr. Cleary, rest assured you will be reported. I will NOT stand for disrespect in my court merely because you think that you are immune. You WILL accord me the respect I am due or I WILL put you in your place. Do not challenge me on that, sir, or you will be very, very sorry."

"The motion stands," Ron responded coolly.

In obvious frustration, Judge Wilton addressed Carolyn. "Miss Cheline, your responsibility in this matter has ended. You will not bear the brunt of the actions of your supervisor. If I hear that you have, I will endeavor to make reparation. You are ordered to report to me any such treatment. Mr. Cleary, for the record, you are pursuing this matter and you will suffer the full wrath of this Court should I find one iota of misstatement, falsehood, or lie. Do you understand?"

Ron remained as expressionless as Mount Rushmore.

"Mr. Cleary, you will respond," Judge Wilton threatened.

"I will need a short recess to contact Detective Sullivan."

"For what purpose?"

"To verify the contents of his affidavit."

"If you mean to have him read it to verify its contents, so granted. Do not have him contact the inmate. Are we understood?"

"My intention was to have him read the affidavit."

Joe sat appreciative of the Judge's interpretation of 'verify the contents of the affidavit'. He was not leaving Cleary even the weakest of options.

"Contact him and bring him to chambers. Five minutes," Judge Wilton ordered. "Carolyn, you will remain in the courtroom."

Joe G. Continues on

Joe G. had seen the two men about one hour into his surveillance standing near the elevators. He had his two targets. They looked exasperated mulling around the hall and speaking in low angry tones to each other.

Julianne had not yet arrived from her quick appearance on the seventh floor.

He chose then to enter the courtroom in an attempt to catch Joe's eye. Once he had passed through the swinging doors loud voices were audible from chambers. He exited back into the hallway, pushed an elevator button near the two men and listened to bits of their conversation.

"Where the fuck are they?" one said. "How the fuck am I supposed to know?" was the response. "Fuck. Bill ole boy's gonna be pissed. Let's get outta here. I don't think they're gonna have a jury."

Joe exited the elevator on seven and entered the first session. Julianne was just leaving the bar as he looked towards the bench. "What's up, Joe?"

"The two guys are upstairs in the hallway. I just heard them talk about the jury and Bill."

"Where's my father?"

"In chambers. And there's an awful lot of yelling going on."

"Any idea what that's about?"

"No. But I saw that asshole Cleary go in the court room."

"You're kidding," Julianne said excitedly. "Looks like I'm missing all the fun. Does my father have the juror motion?"

"He should. It was on his desk when he left last night."

"Let's take the stairs it'll be quicker. Besides I don't want to run into those two guys in the hallway."

When Julianne entered 8B, Joe was at the defense desk waiting for Cleary to return with Sullivan. They traded information. He instructed Julianne not to come into chambers just yet. "I don't want to introduce you to the Judge. I don't want to throw off the rhythm. What I need you to do is to tell one of the court officers - tell Larry - about the two men. Tell him I'm going to tell the Judge they're here. He's going to want them to be available. See if he will keep an eye on them. Tell Joe to keep an eye on them and follow them if they leave." He reached into his briefcase and handed Julianne his mobile phone. "Give him this so he can call me from wherever he is. Tell Larry about Joe. I'm going to need you to report to the Court. That's when I'll call you into chambers. We've got them on a very serious run. I don't want to let up."

Sullivan didn't like what he was hearing. Ron wanted him to take the heat for this inmate shit. "Ron, you want me to go into that Court and tell the Judge I lied in my affidavit?"

"No. If you say you lied, you say I lied." Ron didn't want to give Wilton any opportunity to slam into him again. He generally knew how far to push. He was real close to the edge. "Just tell him that what you have in the affidavit is an interpretation of what was told to you from the point you first interviewed Mandrake until yesterday."

"Ya, right. And what if he has the visitation log sent over from Charles Street and sees I didn't log a visit?"

"So what. Let him. It won't be enough. If he asks, say you went there but didn't log in because you just wanted to see him for a minute and check if he would still testify. You saw him. You asked him. He said he would. That's it."

"Ron, this is shit."

"I don't care if it's shit. You'll do what I say. You don't have to like it, just do it."

"I have Detective Sullivan in the Court," Ron told Judge Wilton refusing again to acknowledge his position. "He'll explain his affidavit."

"What will he explain?" Judge Wilton asked. "His affidavit speaks for itself."

"He will explain the import of his statements."

"Import? The import of his statements is what is written down and avowed to under the pains and penalties of perjury. Do you want me to give him the opportunity to make further statements under oath?" Judge Wilton asked.

"He is willing to come in here and explain his affidavit to you."

Judge Wilton turned to Trevor and asked him to bring in Detective Sullivan leaning heavily on the word 'detective'.

"Before he comes in I do not want Mr. Balliro to have the opportunity to question him," Ron demanded. "He's willing to make a statement and that's all."

"Mr. Cleary, sit down and keep your mouth shut," Judge Wilton ordered. "I'll decide who will question and what opportunities will be given."

Turning to Joe he said, "Mr. Balliro, if you have a desire to question the detective we will excuse him and I will hear from you, understood?"

"Completely, your Honor," Joe answered.

Detective Sullivan entered behind Trevor affidavit in hand. He stood stiffly, nervously, waiting for direction. "Detective, please identify yourself for the record," Judge Wilton ordered.

"The record?" Sullivan immediately responded. He turned to Ron. "You didn't tell me nuthin' about no record."

"Detective, identify yourself for the record," Judge Wilton ordered again.

Sullivan shook his head back and forth slowly before answering. "Detective Jonathan

Sullivan, Boston Police Department, District A, currently assigned to the Homicide Division of the Suffolk County District Attorney's Office."

Sullivan looked around the room and caught a somewhat irritating curl on the corner of Carolyn's mouth.

"Is there something you want to say to the Court, Detective?"

Sullivan stood there dumbly, not knowing what to do but certain that if he said anything that was different from his affidavit he would substantiate a perjury charge. He didn't trust Cleary. He knew that if anyone would get hurt, he would. "I got nothing else to say than what's in my affidavit."

Judge Wilton turned to Ron in a deliberate manner. "Mr. Cleary, you have wasted enough of the Court's time. Trevor," he called, "prepare a van to take us all to Charles Street immediately. Detective, maybe you want to talk to Mr. Cleary before we go. You are not invited and are ordered to stay clear of the jail and not to contact them by phone until after we leave from our little visit. Do you understand?"

"Yes, your Honor. But I need to talk to Mr. Cleary before you go."

"I will give you that opportunity."

"Your Honor?"

"Yes, Mr. Balliro?"

"I would ask that you order that Mr. Cleary not be permitted to contact Charles Street prior to our arrival."

"Granted, Mr. Balliro. Is that understood, Mr. Cleary?"

"Sure. I understand." Ron responded curtly. Outside the courtroom, Sullivan made his anger known. "Okay, Ron, you want to play games, here's the rules. You give me up, I give you up. That includes everything, all the other shit that's been going on for years. I might not be 'enough to bury you, but it'll raise a stink you won't imagine. You got a lot of balls stickin' me in there under oath. Did you really think I'd trade my pension for you? Fuck you!"

Ron listened without expression. He didn't like threats, especially when they could materialize. "I'm going to withdraw the motion and tell Wilton that Carolyn will renew it once we have verified the witness' availability for trial." He turned to Carolyn who had witnessed Sullivan's the tirade. "You got that, Carolyn. You're not to do anything with this before contacting me."

"Fine. I have no problem with that," Carolyn said relieved she could get back to her trial. As long as the battle lines were drawn between Ron, Sullivan, and the Judge, she didn't mind giving up a little control. She hadn't asked for this and there was no way she was going to voluntarily become part of it.

Feeling vindicated Carolyn turned briskly from the two old boys and walked into the courtroom alone.

Turning to Joe she said, "Motions withdrawn."

Judge Wilton was more than satisfied.

Neither Patrick nor Teddy spoke while the elevator descended non-stop from the eighth to the first floor. They appeared to be suspicious both of Joe and the bulky mobile phone slung across his shoulder. Peripherally he sensed questioning and nodding glances. When the elevator emptied onto the first floor, Joe allowed the two men to take the lead.

There were many routes from the expansive brick plaza of Government Center outside the front door of the court house but only one that most immediately exited the plaza onto the street. Joe followed Patrick and Teddy and most of the crowd to the left. As they walked down the short incline to the street, he remained behind slowly decreasing their distance ultimately catching up and passing them as they squeezed through the wrought iron gate that prevented cars from driving up the emergency access.

Cambridge street offered another choice - left or right - both directions harboring public phones. Joe intended to stop at either phone whichever direction he chose even though he carried the mobile unit. The grossly different rates charged for their respective uses would raise no suspicion and in fact might give reason to the curious eye for his leaving the courthouse. If he chose the wrong direction, he would be in position to view Patrick and Teddy for some time as they walked down the fairly broad and fairly unrestricted expanse of Cambridge Street. If he chose their direction, he would watch them as they traveled up Cambridge Street and again move to follow if they passed from his sight.

Joe took a left guessing that if they had parked on the street they most probably parked in this area where there were a greater number of metered spaces. As he stopped at the phone, Patrick and Teddy passed him and entered a blue Chevy parked two or three spaces ahead. Joe noted the license plate as they drove off.

Phoning the office, he reported his intent to retrieve his car from the garage and to proceed to Southie confident in the belief he would locate them in short order.

By 10 a.m. Bill's discomfort at the previous day's dismissal of the four jurors and his certainty that he had been the cause had developed into a controlled panic. Convinced that he was the subject of today's delay he paced the jury room like an expectant father. With the room divest of the normal friendly banter, an after effect of the loss, the remaining jurors sat quietly unknowingly reinforcing Bill's anxiety. By noon, he was out of his mind with anxiety. Frantically he sought a way out of jury duty testing manufactured excuses for their fortitude visualizing each presentation to the judge. If he was in serious trouble he might be able to circumvent punishment by offering resignation before being discovered. He was certain, absolutely certain that Teddy and Patrick had been taken into custody and perhaps even now were confessing, implicating him in the hope of leniency.

He inhaled deeply and approached the closed door of the juror room. Eleven people watched him with incredulity as he raised his fist and with a sharp rap on the door called the court officer. The door opened and Mike asked what was needed. "I hafta speak to the Judge," Bill said.

"Now," Mike responded.

"Ya. I can't go on. I hafta ask if he can let me outta this trial."

Mike looked at him in disbelief. "Sir, maybe you don't understand. If he lets you go then the trial is over. He needs twelve people. You better have a damned good reason for wanting to get out or you are going to make one very unhappy judge."

"Oh, ya, right. Well, let me think. Maybe I can go on."

"I think you better consider that, sir."

"Ya, okay, let me think."

Mike smiled a little and closed the door.

Bill had forgotten that they needed twelve people. Well, he thought, they ain't going to throw me off because then the trial would be over. And if I'm in trouble, he surmised, then it won't matter because they'll keep me on the jury anyway. He sat down in an uneasy relief.

Mike called Wade on the courthouse extension. "Wade, its Mike. I think we might have a real problem up here."

"Mike, we've got a real problem down here. The Judge is pissed."

"Well, he's going to get more pissed. I just had a juror ask to speak to him about getting off the jury."

"Christ. Who wants to get off?"

"Mr. Lonnegan."

"Well, I'll tell him but I hope he doesn't shoot the delivery boy."

"Just tell him this guy Lonnegan asked and then said he would think about it. He should know he might want off but the guy said he'd think about it."

"Oh, that's a little better. Maybe he won't shoot me. Maybe he'll just break my leg."

"Yeah. Tell him I keep you updated if there's another request."

"Yea," Wade agreed dejectedly.

Chapter 22
Get that C.I. ready

The increase frequency of the 500 mg. ampicillin drip, the 25 mg. of prochlorperazine and the continued use of nikethamide and hydrocortisone sodium succinate and nebulized dexamethazone, although increasing blood gases, preventing nausea and vomiting, and retarding infection, would serve to do nothing to prepare Charlie for trial. In addition, Dr. Ablow was want for a more conservative treatment over an extended period so as to limit the expectant chronic lung disease that Charlie would have to endure for the rest of his life. The more immediate concern was preventing stridor secondary to existent laryngeal edema. A thracheostomy at this juncture would put him completely out of the picture for trial. No one can testify with a breathing tube sticking out of their throat. As long as he continued the aminophylline and nebulized salbutamol it should control airway obstruction and hopefully curb irritation. In a nut shell he couldn't see how this patient could testify and how he, as a doctor, could justify submitting him to the rigors of a trial. While in the throes of this ethical dilemma his secretary informed him that District Attorney Carolyn Cheline was on the line.

"How's the patient?" Carolyn asked.

"Miss Cheline, I don't know how you expect this man to testify in your case. He awoke briefly two hours ago and immediately went into trauma. He can't talk, it's apparent that he doesn't recognize his surroundings, and he was extremely agitated - agitated to the point that restraint was required."

"Doctor, I'm not going to need him for at least another day. Will he be able to be transported?"

"I don't have an answer for you. He is sedated and under a plethora of medication to control infection and the like. Even if he were able to be transported, it is highly unlikely that he would be able to take the stand and testify. He is simply a very, very sick and damaged individual."

"Doctor, I need him. I accept all responsibility. I'd ask that you do not sedate him. The fact that he is taking medication for infection is okay. I just don't want to have to deal with mind altering drugs."

Before Dr. Ablow was able to respond his secretary informed him that Mr. Bottatelli was awake.

"Miss Cheline. That was my secretary. It seems that your witness and my patient has just regained consciousness again. You are welcome to come down here and draw your own conclusions on his competency."

"I'm on my way," Carolyn said grateful to be able to take advantage of the current recess.

After informing the Court that she would be leaving to speak with her key witness and that she was withdrawing the current renewed motion to permit the testimony of the inmate informant, Carolyn collected her yellow legal pad, her gold Cross pen, car keys and law clerk and drove the short distance to the Massachusetts General Hospital.

The presence of his other self had had a calming effect on Charlie. As he regained consciousness he had been assured that somehow he would be protected and that the confusion would be explained. He did feel sluggish though as he turned his head to view the room and stopped to peer at Cheryl sitting in the corner. That person had risen when he looked at her and picked up the phone on the table next to him. He could just barely make out her words, but could feel the soothing nature of her approach. "No threat here," he was assured.

Cheryl saw him attempting to form words through his parched throat but could make out little of what he said. "Don't try to speak, Mr. Bottatelli. The doctor is on his way. Just relax. You're going to be all right." She had placed her hand on his arm and over the restraint hoping that he would think that she and not the cloth strap was holding him down. She was afraid he would rebel against the restraints and she was too tired to physically hold his upper body against the mattress.

At that moment Dr. Ablow and Dr. Shepard entered the room. "Ah, Mr. Bottatelli, I see you've come back to us," Dr. Ablow said purposely stepping in front of Cheryl and replacing her hand with his. "I'm not going to ask how you are feeling because I am sure you are not feeling quite well, but I do want to ask you some questions and you can just nod up and down for a 'yes', and back and forth for a 'no'. Do you understand?"

This is easy, I can do this. He was self-assured - a new confidence. Charlie nodded his head up and down.

"Excellent, Mr. Bottatelli. Now, I'm going to explain what happened and I want you to tell me if you understand. You've had an accident and you are at the Massachusetts General Hospital. Do you understand?"

Charlie nodded yes.

"Great. Now this hospital is..."

The door to the room opened and Carolyn, accompanied by her law clerk, entered the room.

Dr. Ablow turned to her. "Our patient is awake, Miss Cheline and I am asking him a few questions. Would you care to watch?"

"Yes, I would," Carolyn responded.

Turning back to Charlie Dr. Ablow continued. "Now, Mr. Bottatelli, this hospital, the Massachusetts General Hospital. Do you know what city it is in?"

Charlie nodded yes.

"Is it in Washington?"

Charlie nodded no.

"Chicago?"

No.

"Boston?"

Charlie nodded yes.

"Excellent. You are right. Now, do you remember your first name?"

Charlie nodded yes.

"Is it Charlie?"

"Yes."

"Good. Now you have been here for about two weeks. Do you remember what time of year it is? Is it winter?"

Charlie nodded no.

"Is it fall?"

Charlie nodded yes.

"That's right. Now do you think if I gave you a pen and paper you could write down what you remember about what happened to you?"

Charlie hadn't thought about what had happened. He didn't react to the doctor's question right away having to ask his other if he knew what he should say.

"Mr. Bottatelli. Do you remember what happened to you?" Dr. Ablow repeated.

Charlie nodded yes before he could be filled in on the details.

"Miss Cheline, may I borrow your assistant's pad and pen for a moment?"

"Absolutely," Carolyn said reaching towards the law clerk and handing Dr. Ablow the large yellow pad and Bic pen.

"Okay. Let's remove this restraint," Dr. Ablow ordered.

"Mr. Bottatelli, are you right-handed?"

Charlie nodded no.

"Okay. Remove this restraint," he ordered pointing to Charlie's left.

"Mr. Bottatelli, we are going to remove this strap. Please try to remain calm. We'll raise your bed so you can write, okay?"

Charlie nodded yes.

Charlie wrote down what he had been told: I FELL IN THE KITCHEN. His writing was child-like but legible.

Dr. Ablow lifted the pad so Carolyn could see it.

"That's partially correct, Mr. Bottatelli. The reason you fell was because you inhaled some gas and it caused you to pass out. That's why your throat hurts. But don't worry about that. We'll take care of that now that you're awake. We are going to leave now, and I want you to try and get some rest. We'll take off the other restraint so that you can get comfortable. I'll see you again when you wake. Okay?"

Charlie nodded yes, grateful to be released from his awkward position and happy to be left alone.

Dr. Ablow beckoned everyone to the exit and into the hallway. "Well, that's encouraging," Carolyn said holding the yellow pad.

"It may very well be encouraging, but I don't hold out much hope that he will be able to testify tomorrow or the next day for that matter."

"I have to agree with Dr. Ablow," Dr. Shepard said. "He may be unconscious for some time. This little conversation had to have taken its toll."

"I'm sorry Miss Chelinc, but it will be physically impossible for Mr. Bottatelli to speak for some time."

"Understood. But he can write. He's just demonstrated that. That will be enough."

"If he can remember enough to help you," Dr. Ablow added.

"Well that's what I intend to find out. I am going to need access to him for a brief interview the next time he wakes. I won't need much time, and I promise I will not tax him. But I have to find out if he can testify in accordance with his prior statements."

"We'll do the best we can but it is really up to Mr. Bottatelli and his physical condition," Dr. Ablow responded.

"Understood," Carolyn said in much better humor.

When Carolyn returned to the courthouse, she stopped briefly at her office and instructed her law clerk to inform Ron that the motion had been withdrawn and that Bottatelli had woken and was able to communicate. She then walked the short distance across the hall to the courtroom to check on the status of the trial.

Chapter 23
Just Cannot Extricate Himself

"Carolyn?" Trevor called as she entered the room, "Good, the judge needs to speak to all counsel."

"What's up now?" Carolyn responded.

"One of the jurors wants out."

"Jesus. What the hell is going on?"

"Don't know."

"Joe," Trevor called to Joe as he entered the room. "We got another conference with the judge."

"Oh. Okay, let's go," Joe said.

Judge Wilton was seated, leaning back in his swivel chair with his hands folded on his stomach as they entered and sat down. He appeared disgusted and frustrated. "I have been notified that one of the jurors, a Mr. Lonnegan, may be seeking dismissal from the jury. I don't know why and I don't care. I will not release him unless he represents to me dire circumstances."

"Your Honor, has he specifically asked for release or just indicated he may?" Joe asked.

"He has indicated that he will think some more before he makes his request."

"And that is Mr. Lonnegan?" Joe asked.

"Yes, Bill Lonnegan."

Without hesitation, recognizing a golden opportunity, Joe divulged his investigation. "Your Honor, based upon this latest development, I feel that this would be the appropriate time to reveal to the Court that I have been conducting an ongoing investigation into what appears to be some sort of scheme to disrupt the integrity of the jury."

Taking a minute to absorb this sudden revelation Judge Wilton said in earnest: "Mr. Balliro, perhaps you had better explain."

"Yes, well," Joe began, "I grew suspicious of this particular juror after being informed by my father that he appeared to be impatient, moving around a lot, and appeared to be very animated in reaction to the proceedings. As I have done in the past, I requested my private investigator to do a cursory background examination of Mr. Lonnegan. That investigation revealed that he is William Lonnegan. His father was killed some 30 years ago in the North End of Boston. No one has been indicted or charged in that murder. Obviously, Mr. Lonnegan lied on the questionnaire. I then requested further investigation after the incident with the four jurors yesterday. Mr. Guidetti, my investigator, went into the local neighborhood where Mr. Lonnegan lives and learned that Mr.

Lonnegan and indeed the whole neighborhood holds the defendant out as guilty. In fact, the defendant is blamed for the injuries to the juror that has left him with a limp that is apparent on close examination of his gait."

"Moreover, today, in the hallway outside the courtroom, Mr. Guidetti has observed the two men who were in the elevator and I believe is as of this moment tailing them. I believe one of your court officers has been notified of their presence. Your Honor, it is my belief that somehow this juror, Mr. Lonnegan, has entered into some type of conspiracy or pact with these two men to prejudice this jury against the defendant. I don't know the extent of the harm done, if any, nor do I have a plausible suggestion on how to proceed, but I do find it most interesting that at this juncture, the day after you have released four of the jurors, Mr. Lonnegan is contemplating a request to be excused."

As Joe revealed Bill Lonnegan's probable complicity in jury tampering, Carolyn had become more and more agitated and anxious to respond. "Your Honor, I object most strenuously to Mr. Balliro's interference with the jury. He was well aware of the potential, as he states it, that Mr. Lonnegan may have violated the precepts of juror confidentiality when he argued to have the four jurors excused. He has utilized, improperly, information he alone had to place his client in a strategically advantageous position for mistrial. He had absolutely no right to conduct his own investigation into any of the jurors once they had been selected. He could have challenged him and he didn't. Now he has to live with it."

"All right, all right people," Judge Wilton interjected. "Mr. Balliro, I recognize your concern about Mr. Lonnegan. There does seem to be more than meets the eye with respect to that man. However, I must agree with Miss Cheline that the proper time to have disclosed your discomfort with him was yesterday prior to my dismissal of the four other jurors."

"Perhaps so, your Honor. Yet I did not for a very good reason. I did not have any support for alleging misconduct on his part until last evening. In addition, I am not asking for his dismissal nor am I asking that you inquire of him. At least at this point. I would very much prefer to hear the remainder of the Commonwealth's case and present my request for a directed verdict. I do not want a mistrial. I do not want my client to remain incarcerated while the Commonwealth re-indicts and seeks another trial. It was, and is my judgment that until such time as I am able to establish a more concrete link between these two men and Mr. Lonnegan this Court would not have the justification for dismissing the jury and declaring a mistrial."

"Your Honor, I ask that you order Mr. Balliro to cease and desist from any further investigation into Mr. Lonnegan and the alleged two men."

"No, Miss Cheline. I am not going to make that order. Mr. Balliro, I would ask that you have a complete report available to me tomorrow morning. I will allow you to continue your investigation until that time and will decide then whether to terminate that investigation. I am also going to put one court officer in the presence of Mr. Lonnegan at all possible times. That will serve to stifle any improper remarks by Mr. Lonnegan if he is inclined to do so. I would note however that if it is indeed the purpose of Mr. Lonnegan to infect the minds of the jurors towards a guilty verdict he cannot do so if he is not on the jury. Therefore, his request to be excused is inconsistent with that goal."

"Understood, your Honor," Joe responded.

"Your Honor, do you have objection to my office conducting its own investigation?"

"No, Miss Cheline, but if you do so I'd ask that you supply me with a report as well."

"Understood."

"Now, let's get back to trial. Miss Cheline, when should we expect your key witness?"

"Tomorrow morning."

"Who do you have for us today?"

"The medical examiner. Dr. Shepard."

"How long do you expect he will take?"

"The rest of the day."

"Well can't we quicken up his testimony through stipulation. Mr. Balliro, do you agree the victim died in the manner as has been described in discovery."

Before Joe could answer, Carolyn exercised her prerogative. "Your Honor, the Commonwealth will not agree to any stipulation with respect to this witness. We request the right to present his complete testimony, including his background, to the jury."

"Okay, Miss Cheline. Then let's get on with it."

Joe G. Muscles Up a Little

Joe G. had learned over the years that unless you had two cars it was almost impossible to successfully tail somebody without getting caught. It was just too obvious. It was clear that Patrick and Teddy knew they were being tailed. After five of the last ten minutes driving obvious circuitous routes to ensure to themselves they were being followed, they had pulled to the curb intending to act nonchalant forcing Joe to pass.

It was time for a Joe G. no-holds-barred, no nonsense, face to face confrontation. Joe turned left anxious to navigate around the block and pull in front of their car as it remained parked at the sidewalk. As he turned back onto "D" Street, he saw the car pull out and up to the stop sign. Joe unabashedly pulled up behind them. Sighting Joe, Patrick and Teddy turned the corner and again pulled over to the curb. This time Joe pulled out in front of them immediately exiting his car with his jacket open and his gun in plain view. "Okay gentlemen, you want to turn the car off and get out?" he announced.

"Who the fuck are you?" Teddy demanded.

"I'm a private investigator hired by Joe Balliro to investigate you two and Bill Lonnegan." Joe could see he struck a nerve.

"Yeah, so?" Patrick said.

"So I think we better have a talk because I've got to report to the judge and I'll do it with or without your input. Understand?"

Patrick and Teddy looked at each other. Patrick turned off the car, exited, and slowly walked over to Joe's car. Teddy followed.

Chapter 24
Trial

"Dr. Shepard, do you have an opinion based on your training, skill, and experience, your investigation of the tests and reports you have testified you have reviewed, and based upon your examination of the body of Mr. Francone, as to the cause of death?" Carolyn asked.

"Yes, I do," Dr. Shepard responded.

"What is that opinion?"

"That the deceased, Anthony Francone, died from loss of blood due to massive trauma to his knees and the arterial vessels in his upper left leg and secondary from the trauma inflicted about his face, specifically his lips, tongue, nose, and eyes."

"Do you have an opinion as to what caused the trauma to his legs and upper thigh?"

"Yes."

"What is that opinion?"

"That the trauma to Mr. Francone's knees and upper left thigh were caused by the sudden application of a hard sharp instrument in a short static movement carrying downward from the upper part of the leg over the knee cap."

"And have you come to an opinion as to when that trauma was caused?"

"Yes."

"When?"

"Your Honor, can we have a more specific question?" Joe asked.

"Well, I think Miss Cheline is talking about whether the injuries were inflicted before or after Mr. Francone was tied to the post. Am I correct?" Judge Wilton said directing his attention to Carolyn.

"Yes, your Honor. Thank you."

Turning to Dr. Shepard he said: "You may answer the question doctor, if you can."

"The trauma was inflicted after Mr. Francone was tied to the post."

"Why did you come to that opinion, doctor?"

"That opinion is based on the trauma to the skin around that area. Mr. Francone reacted violently to the infliction of the trauma to his legs as is evidenced by the severity of skin abrasions and lacerations characteristic of wounds caused by ropes or other types of hemp like restraints."

"And do you have an opinion as to what caused the wounds inflicted around Mr. Francone's face and mouth?"

"Yes ma'am."

"What is that opinion?"

"Your Honor, I renew my motion," Joe interjected.

"Denied. Your rights are preserved," Judge Wilton responded.

"That the trauma around the face and mouth of Mr. Francone was caused by large wharf rats."

The jury shuddered collectively.

"How did you come to that conclusion?"

"The wounds had a distinct signature indicating that they were inflicted by teeth. In addition, tests revealed the presence of rodent saliva at and among the wounds."

The jury again shifted uncomfortably.

"Your Honor, may I approach the witness?"

"Yes, Miss Cheline."

"Doctor, I show you a series of photographs. Can you identify them?"

"Yes, counselor. They are photographs taken in my presence at the autopsy of Mr. Francone."

"And are they a fair and accurate representation of what they portray?"

"Yes, counselor."

"And I show you what had been marked as Commonwealth's Exhibit for identification number 23. Can you explain what it is a photograph of?"

"Objection, your Honor. The documents speak for themselves," Joe said.

"No. I'm going to allow him to explain given that they are not something that the jury may be inherently familiar with."

"That is a photograph of the deceased's mouth and face area showing the wounds inflicted by the rodents."

"And this picture, doctor?"

"That and this photograph show the trauma to the knees, thigh, and leg area of Mr. Francone."

"Your Honor, I offer Commonwealth's exhibits 23, 24, and 25."

"I object," Joe said. "On the basis previously noted to the Court."

"Overruled. They are admitted."

"May I publish them to the jury?"

"Yes, Miss Cheline."

Carolyn first approached defense table and offered the pictures to Joe for inspection. Joe took them without fanfare leaning across in front of Tony to share them with Julianne. He purposely looked askance at the shots with disgust. He beckoned Carolyn within range of a loud whisper and said sarcastically, "You sure you've got the most revolting pictures in the bunch", making sure the jurors heard the word revolting. Carolyn reached for the pictures without comment. Looking at the Judge, she walked over to the side of the juror box and handed the photographs to Trevor who then passed them to the jury foreperson to be viewed and passed along.

The effect on each member of the jury was obvious. Some held the photos by their edges as if to avoid contamination. Others passed them quickly only glancing briefly at the gruesome display. All shook their heads in disgust or grimaced in shock. The color on the faces of some changed radically. Trevor stood nearby with fresh water and a mindful eye towards those who appeared to have a fragile constitution.

Joe tried to gauge by reaction which of the jurors might hold the forced viewing of the photos against the Commonwealth.

Bill kept his reaction close to the vest afraid that he was being watched. That lack of reaction made Joe more suspicious than he would have been had Bill reacted with disgust and stared at Tony.

Carolyn waited patiently before continuing her examination of the doctor flipping through her notes. She wanted to give the jury time to absorb her most potent visual aids.

Tony leaned back in his chair obstructing the jury's view with Joe's body.

Julianne unabashedly watched the jury occasionally catching the eye of a juror who glanced toward the defense table her face an expression of sympathy.

"Please continue, Miss Cheline," Judge Wilton ordered when the last of the pictures were in the hands of the last of the jurors.

"Yes, your Honor," Carolyn said. "Doctor, you've testified that the victim died from massive loss of blood due to trauma inflicted by ..."

Joe stood and interrupted. "Your Honor, may we have a question and not a summary of his testimony?"

"Miss Cheline, get on with it," the Judge ordered.

"Doctor, how long did it take for Mr. Francone to die?"

Joe stood again. "Your Honor, is my sister asking for an opinion?"

Judge Wilton took over. "Doctor, in your opinion how long did it take for Mr. Francone to succumb to his injuries?"

"In my opinion the victim succumbed approximately six to eight hours after being tied to the post."

"Now, Doctor, do you have an opinion of how long Mr. Francone would have been conscious during that six to eight hours?" Carolyn continued.

Joe waited for the next question to object.

"Yes, I do," Dr. Shepard said.

"And how long would he have been conscious during the six to eight hours it took him to die?"

"Objection."

"Your Honor, I am offering this on cruel and atrocious," Carolyn argued.

"Understood. Objection overruled."

Dr. Shepard continued. "In my opinion Mr. Francone would have been conscious from anywhere upwards of four to six hours of the six to eight he was alive. Roughly two thirds of that period."

"On what do you base that opinion?" Carolyn asked.

"That opinion is based upon the discovery of a substantial amount of a drug commonly known as speed in the decedent's blood. This substance would have insured that Mr. Francone remained conscious long enough to be cognizant of his surroundings and of his pain until the loss of blood became so substantial so as to cause him to pass out."

"Your Honor, I move to strike so much of that response that deals with what Mr. Francone would have known and felt," Joe motioned.

"Denied, I find it within his field of expertise."

"So that basically, Doctor, someone intended that Mr. Francone experience his own death?" Carolyn asked.

Joe shot up out of his seat, "I pray your Honor's judgment. That was a totally improper question and I move that it be stricken."

Judge Wilton reacted simultaneously. "Miss Cheline, you know better than that. That question is stricken and the jury is instructed to disregard it."

"Doctor, could Mr. Francone have injected himself with the drug called speed?"

"Objection again, your Honor."

"Miss Cheline, I'm not going to allow you to get into speculation with this witness. Now, if you have some foundation for this line of questioning or an offer of proof I'll hear you at side bar. Otherwise, get on with it."

With practiced judgment Carolyn decided not to pursue this line of questioning and settled with the hope that she had been successful in emphasizing the cruelty of the murder on the jury and that others had committed the murder.

"I have no more questions of this witness at this time your Honor."

Judge Wilton turned his attention towards Joe inviting cross examination. Before Joe could start, the Judge inquired of the jury if they needed a recess. One juror asked for a glass of water. While waiting, Joe asked Julianne to contact the office and find out the status of Joe G.'s investigation.

Joe had a limited cross examination for the doctor principally because Carolyn had left open the gap between when the transcript had indicated Tommy was supposed to be killed and when the time of death was fixed by Dr. Shepard. Carolyn had seemingly felt that this was not important enough to highlight perhaps fearful that a battle over this issue would draw the focus of the jury.

Doctor Shepard had testified that at the latest Tommy had been inflicted with the wounds to his legs after being tied to the post sometime between 12 midnight and 2 a.m. on March 3rd. Joe still had the 26 to 28 hour unexplained time period.

"Doctor, it is your testimony, is it not, that Mr. Francone was left at the pier sometime between the hours of 12 midnight and 2 a.m. on March 3rd?"

"Yes, that would be correct. He had to have been tied to the post in that time frame. That's not when he died, that is when he was tied to the post."

Before asking the next question Joe gave the doctor a look of intolerance. A warning that any attempt to design his responses to the benefit of the Commonwealth would not be tolerated. "Understood Doctor. I understand that it is your testimony that he was left at the pier," Joe accentuated with quotation marks in the air before continuing, "sometime between the hours of midnight and 2 a.m. on the day of March 3rd. . ."

"Yes, tied to the post," the doctor added treading carefully in response naturally suspicious of Joe.

"Understood, doctor, we've got that part of your testimony, don't we? You mean 'tied to the post'," again Joe purposely mimicked with quotation marks this time with surely manner.

"Objection, your Honor," Carolyn said.

"Overruled. Okay people; let's keep this on a polite basis. Doctor, just answer the questions yes or no. If you can't answer the question yes or no, say so and I will instruct

287

Mr. Balliro to rephrase. Otherwise do not editorialize."

"Yes, your Honor," Doctor Shepard responded.

Joe had gotten the intended effect. It was obvious the witness was far less combative and antagonistic with Carolyn than with he. It was hoped the jury would see that the way a person answers a question is as important as what he says. The doctor definitely was an employee of the Commonwealth.

"Doctor, it is your testimony, is it not, that the wounds to Mr. Francone's legs were inflicted after he was tied to the post."

"Yes, it is the only plausible series of events."

"But you certainly cannot tell us when, after he was tied to the post, the trauma was inflicted, right?"

"No, I cannot," Doctor Shepard agreed.

"In fact, the best you can tell us is that some six to eight hours after the wounds were inflicted, not after he was tied to the post, he succumbed, right?"

Dr. Shepard shifted uncomfortably, unsure of how he testified on direct. "Yes, that's true."

"So when you testified on direct that Mr. Francone succumbed to his injuries six to eight hours after being tied to the post what you really meant to say was that he succumbed six to eight hours after his injuries, right?"

"Yes, that would be correct."

"Now doctor, you make observations after the fact and attempt to recreate what happened, isn't that correct?"

"Generally that's a safe assumption of the procedure, although more complicated," The doctor interjected.

"You certainly were not present when Mr. Francone was tied to the dock, were you?"

"No, I was not."

"In fact, Doctor, you cannot testify as to when the drug you have called speed was injected into Mr. Francone, can you?"

"Well, not really."

"Incidentally, Doctor, I note that you have little or no background in toxicology, do you?"

"No, I do not."

"So that you have relied on another person's report concerning the presence of this drug speed, am I right?"

"Yes, I have, sir."

"Did you speak with that person?"

"No, I did not."

"In fact the only thing you rely on in making your opinion as to the drug you have testified to, is one line in a standard toxicological rundown of the deceased's blood indicating the presence of methylphenethylamine, correct?"

"Yes. That and a research text."

"Oh. And a book? You looked it up, right?"

"Well to verify my understanding of what the drug was."

"I see. And when you looked it up, the book told you that this amphetamine is commonly known as speed?"

"Well not exactly. The effects as described in the book indicated the drug has the same properties and therefore would cause to be exhibited the same symptoms as what is commonly known as speed," he explained.

"Well Doctor, then the amphetamine that you read about being found in Mr. Francone's blood is not commonly known as speed, right?"

"It would be more exact to say that it would create the same reaction as what is commonly known as speed."

"Of that you are absolutely sure, Doctor, right?"

"Well, no not absolutely, but within a reasonable degree of medical certainty."

"But certainly not a certainty?" Joe reiterated emphasizing the last word of his last question.

"No. Not with a certainty."

"Thank you, your Honor, I have nothing else," Joe said addressing the Court.

"Any redirect, Miss Cheline?"

"Yes, your Honor, one question," Carolyn said turning toward the doctor, "Your opinions are based upon a reasonable degree of medical certainty, correct, Doctor?"

"Yes, counselor. And on my training, experience, and review of all applicable data."

"And that opinion, Doctor, is that Mr. Francone died of ..." Carolyn was interrupted.

"We are not going to review the whole direct, are we, your Honor?" Joe said.

"No, we are not. Miss Cheline, you are finished, are you not?"

"Yes, your Honor. I have nothing else of this witness," Carolyn said nodding toward the Doctor.

"Thank you, Doctor. You may step down," Judge Wilton explained to Dr. Shepard.

Once the doctor had left the stand and the bar area, Judge Wilton announced: "It is now 12:45. We will break for lunch and continue at 1:30. This court is in recess. Please remove the jury."

While the jury was being escorted out of the courtroom, Julianne returned. Joe glanced cursorily at her as she approached counsel table waiting until the jury had exited before making any comment. Before he could ask her what was happening outside the courtroom, the Judge ordered everyone to side bar.

"Who do you have for us this afternoon, Miss Cheline?"

Joe sensed that she was in a pickle and would not have Charlie ready

"Your Honor, given your ruling on the inmate, I do not have anyone available."

"Miss Cheline, forget the inmate. Who do you have left as witnesses for your case?"

"Just the confidential informant, your Honor."

Joe asked, "Is my sister referring to Mr. Bottatelli or another confidential informant?"

"I am referring to Mr. Bottatelli, Mr. Balliro," Carolyn said icily.

"Miss Cheline, I am not going to recess. Get a witness here. If he is your only witness left, get him here."

"Your Honor, that may be physically impossible."

"Why?"

"Because it was not expected that he would be testifying today and he may be under medication."

"Miss Cheline," Judge Wilton started slowly, "you have represented to me that this witness would be able to testify from the outset of this trial. You knew well that trials seldom proceed as planned and that today could very well be the close of your case. I suggest most strenuously that you get him here this afternoon or your case will be in serious jeopardy. Do I make myself clear?"

"Yes your honor, but I had expected that the Court would be considering Mr. Balliro's motions on Mr. Bottatelli 's competency and at the very least that the Court would conduct a voir dire of the treating physician to determine the witness's ability to testify. That is what I expected." Carolyn said attempting to stall for time.

"Your Honor," Joe said, "as you recall those motions were denied by the Court and I was given leave to renew them at a later date if I saw fit. I have made no further mention of those motions nor do I intend to renew them at this time. I don't know where Miss Cheline's expectations came from but they certainly were not my doing."

"Miss Cheline, get him here or suffer the consequences," Judge Wilton ordered.

"Mr. Balliro, how long do you expect to cross examine Mr. Bottatelli?"

"I expect that he will be on the stand until sometime tomorrow."

"Your Honor," Carolyn responded, "if that is true would the Court consider starting fresh in the morning?"

"No, the Court wouldn't. Get your witness here Miss Cheline. Understood?"

"Yes, your Honor," Carolyn relinquished.

"We reconvene in one half hour."

Carolyn turned and left the courtroom leaving her law clerk behind to guard her papers.

A Juror Plot Unravels

"Joe G. is with the two men who were in the courthouse earlier," Julianne explained to Joe during the recess. "They caught him trying to tail them and Joe figured he might as well just confront them. I got all this secondhand from Lois. Joe G. had just hung up before I called. I tried to get him on the mobile phone from here but he must have shut it off. Apparently, they are definitely in cahoots with Bill Lonnegan. They say that he wanted them to say things to the jury that they heard on the news. This Lonnegan guy told them that the judge was keeping things from the jury that he believed they should hear, like the expected testimony of the inmate informant. Both these guys named Patrick and Ted told him that although they had been on the elevator the day before they didn't know that the female juror was on the jury. They thought she was just some jerk. They say they never ran into the jury or wouldn't know if they did. In fact, they said they never saw their friend Bill walking with any crowd of people. Apparently, they were told by Lonnegan that if they saw him with a group of people, it was the Domainio jury. That's about all I've got. Joe G said he would be returning to the office and would put together something to give to the judge if you want. What do you think?"

"I think this is incredible," Joe said. "Not only has the Commonwealth screwed up their case, but they are getting help from a juror. It's amazing how this open and shut case is going into the hopper."

"What are you going to do with the juror issue?"

"I'm going to sit on it for a while longer. At least long enough to see if the Commonwealth can produce Bottatelli this afternoon. If they do, then I want to see if he can testify. After that I think we'll see the Judge before I make a motion for judgment of acquittal. The fact that he will be facing some kind of inquiry into Mr. Lonnegan may carry some weight on the directed verdict. He may not want to face what most probably will be widespread news coverage of a mistrial. Especially if granted on a juror issue."

"Speaking of which," Julianne forewarned, "the news has already gotten wind of this and are huddled outside waiting for you."

"Well, they will have to wait. I'm not going to face them until after the close of the day. I don't want to anger the Judge nor ruin what may turn out to be a gift. Do me a favor; get me a sandwich from the Dandelion. Just tell the press I have to prepare for this afternoon. You can tell them to expect the key Commonwealth witness. You can tell them his name if you want. Okay?"

"Sure dad. I'll be right back."

Julianne exited the courtroom and could immediately be heard reacting to the hunger of the media ensconced in the hallway of the eighth floor.

Chapter 25
A Little Parental Concern

Gaetano Domainio had great faith in Joe. He and his sister Nichole had sat in the rear of the courtroom throughout the past week purposely avoiding detection by his son, by Joe, by the D.A., by court officers or by anyone else, including the media. Indeed, he had taken great pains to avoid discovery by utilizing a simple principle of disguise. To alter your appearance, make yourself ordinary with one obvious distinction. Therefore, Gaetano wore dress pants, loafers, a white dress shirt with a pen in the pocket, a waist length coat, and a Sculley cap. He wore obvious bi-focal glasses and a hearing aid.

Familiar with his son's demeanor, the way he sits, the message he conveys, Gaetano was angry. Had he been anywhere else he would have slapped him resoundingly on the side of his head to knock some of the smart-ass out of him. Gaetano knew enough about people to know that this jury would convict him just because they thought he had been too cocky throughout the trial. Once Tony was convicted, Gaetano would face having to run the family business at the ripe old age of seventy-nine, not a pleasant prospect. He was retired and wanted to remain that way. The role of problem solver and wisdom giver was perfect for his sedentary lifestyle. He was out of the fast lane and did not choose to take the on-ramp if he did not have to. He didn't want to plan strategy and map out the future. He had done his part. He certainly did not want to have to spend his Sundays driving out to Walpole to visit his stupid kid and he did not want to inherit Tony's family, bring up his kids, take care of his wife; he had done that part as well. Stupid shit kid. Gaetano had gone his whole life without taking a heavy hit and what happens to his kid, he's gotta be a hot shot and practically give himself to the cops.

At the very least, if Tony was put away he could make sure he had it easy in the can. He would get one of the suites with television, radio, books, good jobs. He'd be taken care of.

Gaetano had been around long enough to sense something was wrong in the court room. In the corner seat he had occupied since the start of the trial he had a good overview of the proceedings. Today he saw something that disturbed him; something that he felt now required that he reveal himself to Joe. Two men had come into the courtroom during the cross examination of Doctor

Shepard. They stood at the rear of the courtroom not speaking and left when the gallery emptied after the jury had been escorted to the jury room.

Feds. No question about it, Feds. There was no doubt the two men he had seen were either Federal Special Agents or Federal Marshals. In either case, it did not bode well for his son.

As Gaetano got older, his ability to recognize the early signs of assault coupled with having taken no great hits - everything he had gone down on had been small time - gave him added respect among his peers. Yet with all the time that had passed and all the successes he had had in beating the continued invasions upon his family, Gaetano felt acidic bile rise in his throat whenever he viewed agents of the Federal Government hovering like vultures.

Gaetano detested Federal Officers. He understood that the federal agent philosophy of hate personalized was a step in the ladder of success. The agent that hated with the most distinct sincerity showed his dedication to the job and was reviewed as the most complete. He or she would receive more notice, could potentially be put in the most advantageous position to crack the most controversial cases, be given the carte blanche of investigation, and become the much heralded experienced field agent relied on for advice, education, lecturing, addressing, and advancing within.

Gaetano thus had been convinced decades ago that if it weren't for this desire for upward mobility the agent would lose the passion of his pursuit and the treatment of the target less personalized, more professional.

Gaetano's anger, his hate, stemmed not so much from the continued invasion by these strangers, not so much from the attitude that they must humiliate, humble, and denigrate the one arrested to show their dedication, but their refusal to hold him out as intelligent enough to recognize this. To Gaetano these were just stupid people with all the toys and power a rich uncle could give them. He had no interest in buying such stupidity, only to avoid it least it infect those who are struggling to become thinking beings.

Gaetano was sure they had not seen him. He hoped Joe could figure out why they were at the trial. Maybe out-flank them. To that end Gaetano walked around the crowd of news media accosting Julianne and entered the courtroom.

"Hi Jimmy," Gaetano addressed Jim seated alone in the gallery.

Jim, his eyes weakened by age and not expecting a disguise, took a minute before recognizing a friend he hadn't spoken with for years.

"It's me, Jim. Gaetano," he said while removing his scolly cap.

Jim smiled. "Hi Guy. Good to see ya." He looked at Nichole. "Nichole. Hi. You look lovely."

Nichole returned an affectionate, "Hi Jimmy."

"Let me get Joe," Jim said. "Does Tony know your here?" He made a labored move to stand.

"No, Jim don't say nuthin'. I don't wanna be in the way. They gotta pay attention and I don't wanna be no bother."

"Agghh!" Jim shrugged his shoulders palms up. "You ain't no bother." He made no further move to get his son's attention. "How are ya Guy?"

"Pretty good Jim. Ain't got no complaints. Septin' one right now with my son."

"Yes."

"Yeah, well, listen Jimmy," Gaetano said. "I seen some Feds in here -- today."

Jim said nothing.

"In the back of the room," he continued. "Earlier. They're gone now. But they was here though, the muthafucka's. Jesus, mutha-a-God. I hate them muthafucka's. Pompous muthafucka's. I think these assholes are gonna cause problems but I don't wanna bother your kid durin' the trial."

"Well, I can tell him for you Guy. Shouldn't be a problem."

"Great Jimmy. I just don' wanna bother him."

"You think they're here for Tony, Guy?"

"Ah, who knows? These guys are stupid. It don't make sense though that they'd be afta my kid. He gets hooked, he gets life. Nah. They probably wanna see how the rat does. They're always looking to trade off each otha's rats. They probably want Charlie afta he testifies sos they can use him in one'a they're cases." Gaetano paused. "But if ya get a chance maybe you can mention it to Joe. Just sos he knows they're here."

"Sure Guy," Jim said. "I'll tell him. But maybe they're after you?"

"Nah. Not me. I'm an old man. I don't do nothin' nowadays. They want the rat."

"Okay, Guy. I'll tell Joe you saw them."

"Thanks Jimmy. Thanks a lot. You take care. Call me if you need sumpin' - anythin'. Okay ?"

"Sure Guy. Sure," Jim said. "Bye, Nichole."

"Bye, Jimmy," Nichole said.

Gaetano, a true dichotomy, walked to the gallery slowly. He was an old man, hardened through his skin - right through his heart - blackened with hate. Yet for his family, friends, and community he was generous, kind, and forgiving.

Jim had left his pad of steno paper with its large lines at defense table and now searched for something to note down Gaetano's observations, something he could hand to Joe if he did not have the opportunity to speak with him. He reached for the newspaper, the front page screaming of the Domainio hit on the C.I., tore off the bottom of the page and began to write a note. When he finished writing he looked up and saw that his son was still occupied in reviewing the file, so he turned and smiled at Gaetano and watched Nichole for a minute thinking that even at her age she was as beautiful as she had ever been.

Chapter 26
It is the C.I.'s Turn

Charlie sat in Carolyn's office hand cuffed to the chair. Detective Sullivan stood near him. Dr. Ablow had taken the chair directly in front of Carolyn's desk. Dr. Shepard stood at the rear of the room near the door leading to the hall.

Looking like someone had just dragged him through the digestive tract of a shark; Charlie's eyes were embedded deep in his drawn face, his skin pale, his movement slow and not deliberate. Slumped over, dejected, clearly having difficulty staying conscious, Charlie occasionally pulled and tugged at his handcuffs causing them to automatically tighten in animated response to a perceived attempt to escape their bond. Charlie periodically moaned in surrender to their frustrating grip.

Carolyn sat, staring at her key witness, desperately searching for some way out of having to expose this thing to the jury this day. There was no question that Charlie was going to blow this case. He wasn't even past his writing phase and Balliro would raise a big stink when he found out he couldn't verbalize. Carolyn broke the silence after a few minutes.

"Is their anyway he can speak?" She asked Dr. Ablow.

"Ask him," Doctor Ablow suggested with a shrug. "He's not under any medication that could affect his thought."

"Charlie?" Carolyn called out. "Mr. Bottatelli?"

He didn't respond.

Carolyn got up and walked over to her key witness. "Charlie?" she asked with purpose.

Charlie looked up and pulled at the handcuff. Carolyn, thinking that he looked like a trapped animal about to gnaw off its legs, said: "Mr. Bottatelli, it's okay; we can get you out of those." Carolyn turned to Sullivan and ordered him to remove the handcuffs. Deciding it was best to avoid another confrontation; Detective Sullivan reached for Charlie's hands, pulled him roughly up towards him and removed the restraints. Carolyn looked at him and shook her head back and forth before continuing.

"Okay Mr. Bottatelli, how do you feel?"

Charlie waited for direction. Nothing. He had a great pain in his head. It was too loud. He couldn't hear the other over the noise. He looked around motioning for something to write with. Carolyn responded. "No, Mr. Bottatelli, can you just answer me"

Charlie looked at her and in a course whisper uttered a muted: "Hurts."

"Damn it," Carolyn swore, "damn it all to hell. I know it hurts Charlie, but in a few minutes we are going into a court and you are going to have to take the stand and tell the jury that you killed Tommy. Do you remember telling us that?"

"Uh-huh," Charlie said in a raspy whisper surrendering in agreement.

"Great," Carolyn said turning to all in the room. "That's something anyway." She turned back to Charlie. "Are you going to be able to take the stand and tell the jury that Mr. Domainio told you to kill him?"

Charlie looked up at her rubbing his now freed wrists. "Uh-huh," he said in the same raspy whisper.

"If need be I will ask the judge to allow you to write down your answers and I will try to be brief. Do you understand?"

"Uh-huh." Again the raspy whisper.

"Good Mr. Bottatelli. You're doing very well. This won't take long and then you can go back to bed, okay?"

Charlie, with puppy dog eyes, nodded his head up and down.

"You know I'm going to ask the Court to permit me access to Mr. Bottatelli before you put him on Carolyn," Joe explained.

"I figured as much Joe. I'm warning you he has limited speech capability and he doesn't want to talk to you."

"What do you mean limited? Can he testify?"

"He can testify. He's in complete control of his faculties. Of course, if you want to test his ability you can renew your motion and we can voir dire his doctor."

"No, Carolyn. I think access should be enough. Where is he?"

"In my office. As a matter of fact, I expect him to be brought in any minute."

Charlie was brought into the locked and empty courtroom while both Carolyn and Joe were in chambers. Judge Wilton made short work of Carolyn's rote argument against allowing Joe to speak to Charlie before he testified ordering her to allow Joe the opportunity. He also dealt quickly with Joe's request to limit the direct examination of Charlie. Joe requested that the judge prevent Carolyn from questioning Charlie on his hospitalization, his injuries and the like, given the Court's ruling on the inmate informant.

Since Carolyn had no evidence that Tony was responsible for the hit at the Bradford Hotel she would not be entitled to any inference that the defendant was in any way involved. Any testimony from Charlie about what had happened could cause the jury to draw the inference that Tony was responsible. This Joe reasoned to Judge Wilton, was impermissible, would prejudice the defendant, and was irrelevant to the case at hand. Judge Wilton agreed and ordered Carolyn not to get into that area. Of course Carolyn requested that she be allowed to ask the witness if he had been brought to the Court from the hospital in order to explain his appearance and to give him an address. Judge Wilton denied her request without Joe's anticipated objection.

With Joe and Carolyn in chambers, the only other persons present in the court room with Charlie were Detective Sullivan and one other court officer, the officer that had escorted Tony to the defense table. As Tony was being led into his seat, he glanced behind at Charlie sitting with Sullivan. Smiling he turned forward for a short while to permit the officer to remove his restraints. Freed from his shackles he turned back towards Charlie and mouthed the words: "Charlie, my good friend Charlie. What a nice surprise."

As Charlie started to wave back innocently, Sullivan scowled at Tony. "Turn around scumwad and mind ya own business." Charlie huddled down and sat quietly. Tony raised his middle finger at Sullivan and smiled.

As Joe entered the courtroom he spotted Sullivan seated next to a man who had to be Charlie. He asked Carolyn and she verified that he was her key witness. As Joe walked over to talk to Charlie, Carolyn scurried behind him and when within earshot said, "Charlie, this is Mr. Balliro....."

Joe immediately interrupted recognizing that Carolyn had called out to Charlie in a tone that one might use to would address a twelve year old. "I can handle the introduction Carolyn. Mr. Calhoun - Charlie - my name is Joe Balliro. I represent Tony Domainio. I just have a few questions I'd like you to answer."

Carolyn interrupted. "You don't have to answer any of his questions if you don't want to."

"Thank you, Carolyn," Joe said with sarcasm. "I might have forgot to tell him that."

"Anytime, Joe."

"Mr. Bottatelli, will you answer a few questions?"

Charlie sat still looking first at Joe then at Carolyn but did not respond.

"Mr. Bottatelli, Charlie. Can you tell me what you did on March 1st?"

"Tony," he responded.

"Yes, Tony. I represent Tony. Could you tell me what you did on March 1st?"

"Tell Tony I'm sorry," Charlie said in a course whisper.

"What Charlie? I couldn't hear you. What did you say?"

"Tell him I'm sorry," Charlie said.

Joe drew back a little bit stunned by Charlie's response. "I will Mr. Bottatelli. I will. What are you sorry about?"

"It won't happen again," Charlie answered.

"What won't happen again?"

Charlie didn't respond. "Charlie, what won't happen again?" Joe asked again.

Still no response.

"Can you tell me what happened on March 1st Mr. Bottatelli?"

Nothing. Charlie just sat looking past Joe at Tony.

Joe turned to Carolyn. "Would you be so kind to instruct your witness that I will need some kind of response?"

"No, I will not. It's obvious this interview is over. Let's leave it at that."

310

Joe looked at Charlie's clothes, then at his face. Charlie appeared to be trying to look beyond him at Tony. Following his gaze, Joe looked at the back of his client and then to Charlie. Blocking Tony with his body, he forced Charlie to return his attentions. Joe thought for a moment and asked: "Charlie would you like to talk to Tony?"

Charlie's eyes widened in shock. Carolyn was so aghast she stammered out a long "wwwhhhaaat!!" in disbelief. "That's the most outrageous thing I have ever heard," she said vehemently. "You're trying to intimidate my witness and I won't stand for it. I am sure that is sanctionable Mr. Balliro and I intend to inform the Court."

"Fine, Carolyn. But the record will reflect that your witness brought up the subject and that he was watching the defendant and ignoring my questions. My question was the next in natural sequence and only called for a response not actual contact."

"We'll take it up with the judge," Carolyn ended.

"Fine," Joe agreed.

When the court had entered Carolyn asked for side bar. "Your Honor, I submit to you that Mr. Balliro took the opportunity offered by the

Court for access to purposely intimidate the Commonwealth's key witness. He intentionally directed the witness' attention to the defendant and asked him if he would like to speak directly with him. Mr. Bottatelli's reaction was one of fright. I am asking, therefore, that we recess for the day so that I might have time to calm the witness down in preparation for his testimony."

Judge Wilton looked past Carolyn to Charlie seated next to Detective Sullivan. "Carolyn, your witness does not appear to be in any great distress." Charlie was looking at the ceiling.

"Mr. Balliro, what have you got to say?"

"Your Honor, Mr. Bottatelli brought up the subject of the defendant asking that I relay a message of apology to him. When I tried to continue the interview the witness had a very benign, fixed gaze on the defendant. It was natural to ask whether he wished to speak with the defendant given his attention was directed toward him and given that he was not responding to my questions. I was entitled to that response under the conditions of the interview. And it is because of the condition of the defendant that I must now ask that the Court direct a voir dire of the witness to determine his competency."

Judge Wilton raised his hand to stop Carolyn's immediate response. "You are renewing your motion, Mr. Balliro?"

"Not really, your Honor. I am asking that you conduct a brief investigation into this man's ability to recall, recant, and testify based upon a legal premise as opposed to a medical opinion."

"I object totally, your Honor," Carolyn said realizing that she had been short circuited in her effort to exhaust the day with a voir dire of Dr. Ablow. "If it is Mr. Balliro's intention to renew his motion or to move for an evaluation of this man's competency, I ask that I be allowed to prepare and present a complete presentation."

"He is not renewing his motion. He is merely asking that I conduct a short voir dire now," Judge Wilton said looking at Joe for verification of his understanding.

"That's correct, your Honor," Joe assured him.

Judge Wilton motioned for Trevor while stating to both counsel. "That, I will do. Your request for a recess is denied Miss Cheline. Mr. Bottatelli does not appear frightened at the moment. Trevor, hold the jury. We are going to have a short voir dire."

Charlie sat quietly and cowered in the witness stand careful not to rest his eyes at any one spot or on any one person for any great length of time. That woman had told him how the judge wanted to speak to him and that he would have to answer some questions. That didn't bother Charlie. What did bother him was this chair. He had wanted to remain where he was - behind Tony. He didn't like being up there all alone. The man in the black robe had come into the room and one of the men standing near him had helped him up and then told him to sit down again. This was getting very confusing. The man in the robe asked him his name.

"Charlie Bottatelli," he answered in a stronger whisper.

"Yes;" today was Wednesday.

"Yes;" he just came from a hospital.

"Yes;" fell in a kitchen and had been hurt.

"Yes;" he knew a jury would be coming in and he would have to answer questions of the women and the man sitting in front of him.

"I remember what happened those days," Charlie said when asked about the first week of March.

"And you know, do you not, that you are here testify at the Anthony Domainio murder trial, am I right?" Judge Wilton asked.

"Yes, you are right," Charlie said in the same whisper amplified electronically to almost normal speech.

Judge Wilton continued. "Now, you know the difference between a lie and the truth, do you not?"

"Yes, I do."

"If I told you your name was Bill, would that be a lie or the truth Mr. Bottatelli?"

"That would be a lie," Charlie responded.

"Fine, Mr. Bottatelli. How are you feeling?"

"Tired."

"Can you continue today if I bring in the jury?"

"Uh huh."

"Fine."

Judge Wilton turned to both counsel and started to speak. Joe stood up and said, "May I inquire, your Honor?"

"No, Mr. Balliro, you may not. I find that this witness is competent to testify. He has demonstrated sufficient ability to recall, recant, and to relate. He himself has indicated his willingness to continue. Based on his responses I am bringing the jury down and we will continue."

Carolyn reflected on Charlie's performance. Encouraging. At least this afforded him the chance for a dry run without the jury. Hopefully it will have bolstered his confidence. The true irony, Carolyn realized, was that she as a prosecutor was hoping that a jury would feel more sympathy than disgust towards a man that had committed a truly vile murder.

Joe, on the other hand, was suspicious. Something still was not right. He would have to be tactful and strategic in his cross to ferret out that which had eluded the Court and him.

An Relieved and Excited Juror

Bill was pleased when the jury was directed to line up in their prearranged positions at the jury room door because it meant that the trial was to continue. After asking to be excused from the jury, he had chastised himself for his stupidity. He had all but confessed that he was involved in the dismissal of the two jurors, convinced something had happened with Patrick and Teddy. But he also knew the prosecution's case was almost over. They had one big witness left. If the papers and TV were correct, it was the guy that Domainio had ordered to kill Francone. If he could get past that witness he figured nothing would happen to him and he could just either hold out for a guilty or try and convince everyone else. That wouldn't be hard.

"Must be almost over," one juror said to Bill as they waiting to file into court. "I'd just like to get it over. Deliberations won't take long."

Music to Bill's ears. That's two for guilty, he thought. The women won't be a struggle but that nerd brain near the end of the line will want to go over everything. If I can get this guy on my side then we can gang up on the ones that are idiots.

"Yah, this is gotta be the easiest choice any jury will ever hafta make," Bill said. "Our only problem is convincing' everyone else."

The juror in front of Bill nodded in agreement.

<u>Charlie</u>

Charlie's trip to the stand was a Pavlovian entree gladly tossed with abandon to appease the voracious hunger and insatiable appetite of the media. The din of the court room increased noticeably as the print media rumbled and shifted simultaneously, scribbling words in response to their strained glimpses, painting a picture in shorthand of Charlie's slumped bulk as he nervously and obediently following the court officer from his seat to the side of the witness stand.

"Stand over here. Face this way," the court officer ordered attempting to direct Charlie's attention to the bench for his swearing in. Charlie resisted a little. Larry whispered in his ear: "Don't give me a hard time, now. I just need you to face the bench." Charlie did what he was told. He had no intention of resisting; he wanted the show to come out great, except that his legs felt like they were giving out from under him. Larry helped him stand.

"Sir, raise your right hand," the clerk directed. "Do you swear to tell the truth, the whole truth, and nothing but the truth, so help you God?"

Charlie looked at Carolyn, looked at the court officer and in a raspy, whispered voice said: "Uh huh."

Judge Wilton motioned to the officer with a wave of his hand indicating the witness's response was sufficient and turned to Charlie. "Sir, we will need you to answer the questions put to you as completely as possible. The court reporter cannot put 'uh huh's' or other commonly used interjections down on paper. Do you understand?"

"Yah."

"Your Honor, perhaps we can have the microphone turned up a little higher so that the jury can better hear the witness?" Carolyn suggested.

Judge Wilton pushed his wheeled high backed great chair to the opposite side of the bench and increased the volume to the speakers above the jury box.

"Mr. Bottatelli, please take the witness stand."

With eyes and head darting back and forth Charlie lowered himself into the chair he did not favor.

"Your right, Joe," Tony whispered to Joe. "He looks fuckin' nutty."

Carolyn now found herself at the proverbial moment of truth. With all the evidence she was able to introduce thus far she still needed a concrete link to Domainio. At the very least she had to establish that Charlie was the confidential informant on the tape, that he was the one that killed Francone, and that he was ordered by Domainio to do so by Tony. As it was always in even the most complicated of prosecutions and for that matter, the most sophisticated of defenses, proof came down to a few key issues of fact without which either side would collapse. Today - now, and in the next moments - Carolyn was to be called to the bar. She was on trial. She must prove her innocence. She must establish the credibility of her case. She must slay the defenses of false accusation, abuse of power, and personal vendetta. To do so, she must convict.

Standing at the podium waiting the court's permission to begin, she looked like an expectant, hopeful gambler in front of an one-arm bandit waiting for the best moment to start the spin of the wheel that would speak fortune or failure. Finally, with a sense of slight trepidation, acknowledging the Judge's grant, Carolyn launched into her direct.

"Thank you, your Honor. Would you please state your name and spell your last name for the record?"

Charlie sat still for a minute. His lips moved but he said nothing. He stopped. A moment later he started again.

"Charlie Bottatelli. . ." Before he could finish, the increased volume caused Charlie's raspy whisper to feedback from the speakers into the microphone and a high pitched shriek emitted violently above the jurors. Charlie jumped up and back, falling out of the small witness box and landing in front of the jury.

Bill, seated in the second row, second seat, above where Charlie had landed covered his face with one hand and shook his head back and forth in disgust. Stupid fuckin' clown, he thought.

Judge Wilton reached to decrease the volume while at the same time Trevor rushed to assist Charlie. "I'm sorry, Mr. Bottatelli," he said. "This system is delicate and causes quite an alarm sometimes. Are you all right?"

No answer. By now Charlie was back on the stand confused and afraid.

"Mr. Bottatelli, are you injured?"

No answer.

"Let me see counsel at side bar."

"Miss Cheline, I must say that no matter how loud that feedback was, I don't believe his reaction was called for. I recognize that I have ruled him competent, but he appears to have regressed. It may just be nervousness but I am beginning to seriously question my own ruling. Are you sure your witness is capable of testifying in this trial?"

"Yes, your Honor, he is. It is probably just the jury and the public. He will gain his confidence again. I do note that he has gone back to a whisper. The voir dire may have taken its toll on his ability to verbalize. He has in my past interviews been very conversant with pen and paper and based on that I would ask that you allow him to write down his answers."

"Mr. Balliro?"

"I object, your Honor. This is the Commonwealth's key witness. A witness that is supposed to put my client in jail for the rest of his life. The jury must be given the opportunity to observe his manner of speech, his demeanor when answering, his facial expressions, the positioning of his body, and by that I don't mean on the floor, and the strength of his convictions in the force of his statements otherwise I submit Mr. Domainio will be denied his right to a fair trial, confrontation and due process of law."

"How do you propose that we proceed, Miss Cheline?"

"I will ask a question. Mr. Bottatelli will be allowed to answer in writing. I will show it to Mr. Balliro first and if there is no objection to the answer I will have one of my assistants read it to the jury."

"I object to that process as well," Joe responded. "First, it will take forever for this witness to testify on direct; second, I object to

Miss Cheline's suggestion that one of her assistants would read the answer. We have no way of controlling the manner of delivery and it is my sense that those answers will be delivered with greater clarity, damnation, and sophistication than this witness could ever muster. Third, if the question of this witness' competency arises again, your Honor will have no ability to evaluate his condition and; lastly this method will seriously undermine my cross-examination essentially imposing substantial control by the Commonwealth over the answers, the speed of delivery, the method of delivery, and the appearance of the witness. There is absolutely no question that this suggestion is an attempt by the Commonwealth to take improper strategic advantage of this witness' inability to testify and will deny the defendant his constitutional rights."

"I recognize your objections, Mr. Balliro, but I don't see how allowing this witness to write his answers down is any different from allowing a person who is mute from testifying. I will allow this witness to write his answers down if necessary. Miss Cheline you will not suggest this method to the witness. If it appears that the witness is not answering the questions I will suggest it to him. You will give Mr. Balliro the opportunity to read the answer before it is submitted to the jury. Finally, the clerk of the session will read the answer to the jury not one of your assistants. Is that understood?"

Both counsel answered affirmatively.

"Your Honor," Carolyn asked, "perhaps if you asked the witness if he can continue and if he can verbalize before I continue it will save time?"

"It may save time, but I will not give the jury any more reason to feel sympathetic towards this witness. Please continue."

Carolyn returned to the podium and continued.

"Now, Mr. Bottatelli, can you give us a brief description of your background?" Carolyn began.

"Objection, your Honor. The witness hasn't answered the first question put to him."

"Sustained. Please state your name."

In a slow raspy voice Charlie stated his complete name.

"Now can you give us a brief description of your background especially in the past ten years?"

"Objection."

"Sustained." Judge Wilton recognized without clarification that the witness could not testify regarding his employment as a hitman for the defendant. To do so would implicate the defendant in crimes he was not charged with. In addition, the jury would have the tendency to convict because they believed the defendant to be a bad person capable of ordering a murder.

Carolyn continued without missing a step. "Mr. Bottatelli, where have you lived during the last ten years?"

Charlie thought for a while. He was alone. He remembered that someone had been helping him and now he felt alone but he could do it. He didn't need any help. He was feeling stronger. "North End," he said his voice a little stronger.

"How were you employed during those ten years?"

"I worked for Tommy." He was feeling stronger. Charlie was actually enjoying himself. The jury watched him as he spoke. Everyone was listening and watching him. He liked to talk.

Carolyn would have preferred that he have said that he worked for Domainio, but she assumed he was testifying in a technical hierarchical sense given that Tommy, the deceased, had been his direct supervisor. Taking this in stride and turning it to her benefit, Carolyn tried for an explanation of the infrastructure of the organization hoping it would give Charlie's testimony a little more sex appeal. "You worked for Tommy. Tommy who?"

This is easy Charlie thought. "Tommy Francone."

"He was your boss?"

"Yeah. He was my boss. I did what he says I do." Astoundingly, Charlie was falling back into character. The underworld hitman was surfacing. There was an astounding transformation from the injured puppy to the frenzied pit bull. Joe turned to Julianne with a smile. "Do you believe this guy? Am I dreaming?"

"Now, Tommy was your boss," Carolyn continued. "Who was Tommy's boss?"

"Objection."

"No. Overruled, Mr. Balliro. If he knows. You may answer, Mr. Bottatelli."

"Okay. He didn't have no boss. He was my boss."

The gallery murmured and shifted. Carolyn paused. That wasn't right. That was a wrong answer.

Joe leaned forward anxiously.

"Maybe you didn't understand, Mr. Bottatelli. Who was Tommy Francone's superior? Who did he take orders from?"

"Objection, your Honor, askcd and answered."

"Overruled," Judge Wilton ordered visibly upset. "Answer the question," he ordered in a less than tolerant tone.

"No boss."

The gallery reacted almost immediately. Members of the media were perched on the edge of their seats readying to launch out of the court room and race for the telephones as soon as it became clear that the rat had turned stand up.

Carolyn was mystified. She paused again at the podium in disbelief. She searched for answers. She could not have been duped by Charlie. He couldn't have set her up. He had been hurt. He had been hospitalized. He had been non-responsive. He had been cowering just a few minutes earlier. He fell out of the stand. Nobody could look that bad on purpose. She wasn't a rookie. It just couldn't have been an act. In a very serious and deliberate manner she asked: "Do you know a man named Anthony Domainio?"

The question pummeled across the room like an anvil dropped from the highest of buildings during five o'clock rush hour. The answer would determine whom the anvil would crush.

Charlie looked at Carolyn, drawing his head back with skepticism and suspicion as if talking to a child. "Tony? Yeah, I know Tony." Charlie paused and in classic mob slang said: "I oughta know the guy, I fuckin' killed him."

Pandemonium. The jury, the gallery, even the court officer commented in shock. Some of the press, taking a chance that there would be no other testimony that could upstage such a devastating response bolted for the door. Judge Wilton raised his voice in demand of silence. Court officers, now composed, repeated the Judge's order at individuals too caught up in the moment to abide by any of the formalities of justice.

Joe sat back in thought. There was no reason to believe that Charlie would deliberately blow his plea. They had him cold and he would never reach parole. There could only be one explanation. Charlie was confused. He thought he had killed Domainio on Francone's orders. He won't be able to identify the defendant. He thinks Francone is on trial. Therefore, he must believe that Tony is Tommy. That's why he was staring at Tony. He thinks its Tommy. No wonder he was petrified when I asked him if he wanted to speak with Tony. Tony is dead.

By now Judge Wilton was in a controlled fury. It was only with great effort that he did not rise and vent his anger on the witness. When calm had been restored he stopped Carolyn's next words with a raised hand. "Mr. Bottatelli, I want you to listen to my question carefully." His tone, clear that he was in no mood for nonsense, held the room to an unsteady anticipation. "I want you to look over at that table," he pointed at Tony. "Do you see the gentleman seated in the middle of the two attorneys?"

"Yah," Charlie answered his voice clearly audible and tinged with the grittiness of a hardened Mafioso.

"Do you recognize that man?"

"Yah."

"Who do you recognize him to be?"

Charlie drew back again. "Is this some kind of trick?" he asked. He turned, looked at Tony, and pointed with his palm up. "That's Tommy. Tommy Francone."

The gallery began to erupt again. Judge Wilton ordered loudly: "I will have quiet in this court room, is that understood?"

The murmur died. Judge Wilton addressed Charlie again. "If I were to tell you that that man you just identified as Tommy Francone is

Anthony Domainio and that Tommy Francone is dead, what would you say?"

"Your Honor, I must object."

"Overruled, Mr. Balliro. Mr. Bottatelli, answer the question."

Charlie was sure it was a trick. He looked at Tony and Tony smiled. Judge Wilton followed Charlie's gaze, caught Tony's reaction stifling it with a riveted steel eye. "Don't look at him," he ordered. "Just answer the question."

Charlie frowned. "Hey look, I don't know what you want from me. That's my boss Tommy. He told me to kill Tony Domainio. I killed Tony Domainio. You want me to say that's Tony. Hows about this - that's Tony's ghost in Tommy's body." He turned to Tony. "Hey, Tony," he called with exaggeration, a smirk, and a thumb jerked towards the bench. "Tommy's fuckin' dead. Tommy's fuckin' capped," he said with a wink.

"That's enough," Judge Wilton said. "That's quite enough and I've had quite enough." Turning to Trevor he ordered: "Get this man off the stand. Ten minute recess. In my chambers counsel."

Judge Wilton was up and off the bench before Trevor could order 'all rise'. As Trevor began to approach the stand, Charlie

330

continued: "What da fucks his problem? I did'n do nuthin. He asks me - I tell him. What da fuck."

Trevor passed Larry, bringing him in tow, and came closer to Charlie. "Sir, keep your mouth shut and step down."

"Fuck you, you piece of shit," Charlie answered.

The jury pulled away in unison.

"Sir, you have to get off the stand now," Larry said reaching for Charlie's arm.

Charlie pulled away from his reach and stood. "Touch me you little prick and I'll break you're fuckin' arm!" In the process of standing, still under the influence of his injuries, Charlie again lost his balance. This time, however, his reaction was violent. As he stood he began to fall. Instinctively, he took small steps backwards to compensate. As he did his ankles struck the bottom rung of his chair slamming it against the inside of the witness box and causing him to fall despite his attempts to grab for the box edge. He landed awkwardly with his lower back against both chair and the sharp edge of the box opening. Charlie recovered for a brief moment, picked up the chair and flung it a Larry yelling, "I WARNED YA YOU SHIT BUM! I WARNED YA!"

The jury was now standing in the juror box huddled toward the opposite end of the fracas. The media scribbled frantically.

Judge Wilton re-entered the court room and seeing the chair, broken, lying in the bar area to the right of defense table, ordered: "Take this man into custody now!!"

Charlie, his limited energy expended in this sudden burst, slumped heavily to the floor, his eyes tucked deeply into his skull. As Trevor and Larry brought him down the two small steps to level floor, Dr. Shepard appeared with stethoscope. A stretcher was ordered and soon the much more tranquil Charlie was taken from the court.

Joe, Julianne, Carolyn, and her assistant followed the Judge into chambers. Tony was escorted roughly to his holding area.

The gallery went insane.

While the court officers had always endeavored to control wayward discussion about an ongoing trial, there were times when it was proper to allow some limited comment among the jurors, especially after a particularly disturbing incident such as had just occurred. There tended to be an overwhelming desire or need to talk about a mutual and simultaneous outrageous experience. More so if it was as radical as Charlie's testimony. Without condemnation, therefore, the jurors were allowed to make such benign conversation as: "Do you believe that?" or: "Wow, finally some excitement!"

Bill on the other hand saw the opportunity to make limited interpretation before the court officers could intervene. "Ahh, he's just a little confused. Anyone could see that he meant he killed Francone and Domainio ordered him to do it. They shouldn'a picked on him. Anyone could see he was sick." Bill noted that most of his co-jurors nodded in agreement.

Trevor placed his hand on Bill's arm. "Sir please do not talk about the case until deliberations have started."

"Okay, Miss Cheline. Who else do you have?"

"Have, your Honor?" Carolyn said somewhat surprised at the Judge's obvious unilateral decision to terminate Charlie's testimony. "I have no others witnesses. Mr. Bottatelli is my last witness."

Joe and Carolyn had taken the two chairs in front of Judge Wilton's desk. Julianne and Carolyn's law clerk sat on the couch against the wall.

Judge Wilton looked at her, leaned back in his chair and let out a slow breath that he had allowed to build up in his mouth bellowing his cheeks. "Mr. Balliro, I sense you have a motion for the court?"

Joe moved to strike the witness' testimony as he had demonstrated a lack of competency, had failed to identify the defendant, and appears to have exhibited no signs of recovery. He did so asking that the Court reconsider its previous ruling that the witness was competent to testify.

"Miss Cheline," Judge Wilton said dramatically, "I do not want to allow Mr. Balliro's motion. God knows we have gone through a lot to get to this point. I do not blame you for what has occurred and I wish the record to reflect what a fine job you have done thus far. You are indeed a credit to your profession. But this does not bode well for your case. I am not saying that it is over, but it certainly changes my perspective, as it must, on what I can safely anticipate will be a motion for judgment of acquittal by Mr. Balliro at the close of your case. I need you to convince me that it would be proper for you to continue your examination of Mr. Bottatelli. Secondly, the witness was unconscious not moments ago and thirdly he mis-identified the defendant.

With all that said if you wish to continue with Mr. Bottatelli, as I said, convince me."

Desperate to save her case, thinking quickly, Carolyn said: "Your Honor, while it is true that Mr. Bottatelli has mixed up the names of the deceased and the defendant it is clear that he has got the incident correct. He has stated that he was ordered to kill, that he did kill, and that he belonged to the Cosa Nostra in the North End. I would submit that at the very least the Commonwealth ought to be allowed to continue with the examination of the witness to determine whether he can also recant correctly all the other facts concerning the tape, the method of the murder, and the communication of the order from the hierarchy of the organization. The jury should then be allowed to draw an inference that while the witness may be confused as to the identity of the defendant, and I would also point out that this witness had undergone significant trauma and that the names 'Tommy' and 'Tony' are quite similar, that you should allow the jury to infer that what the witness means is that the defendant Anthony Domainio ordered the killing of Thomas Francone and that I be allowed to argue to the jury that inference. Your Honor must admit the witness appears much stronger and more sure of himself on the stand and also appears to be testifying in character."

Judge Wilton had listened intently making the lone comment - "unique" - before directing Joe to respond if he wished.

"Tommy Francone is not on trial," Joe started. "The Commonwealth has sought and has been successful in obtaining indictments against Anthony Domainio who was seated between both counsel at defense table. According to this witness there is no Anthony Domainio at all because he killed him. According to this witness the individual seated at defense table is Thomas Francone who is dead. While the Commonwealth has gone to great lengths to prove that Thomas Francone is dead, their own witness puts him alive and well and in the court room. He has not stated that he may not be alive. He has not testified that the defendant may not be dead. He has unequivocally stated that the defendant is dead and that he killed him. This Court can take judicial note of the inconsistencies in the Commonwealth's position. On the one hand Tony is alive and on trial and Tommy is dead. On the other, Tommy is alive and Tony is dead. This is not a question of inference, which I would submit under these circumstances would be totally improper, this isn't even a question of identity, although again I would argue the Commonwealth has not fulfilled its burden if this witness cannot identify the defendant. It is a question of competency. There is no question that this witness has demonstrated a complete lack of competency to testify even to the most basic of facts - the identity of the defendant. To allow the witness to continue and then to allow the jury to draw such an inference as is proposed by the Commonwealth will violate virtually every constitutional protection afforded this defendant by both the Massachusetts Declaration of Rights and the Constitution of the United States."

"Well said, Mr. Balliro," Judge Wilton responded. "I am going to recess. I am going to take argument under advisement. If you wish to submit memoranda do so by five o'clock tonight. Miss Cheline I'd advise you most strongly to re-assess your position. Mr. Balliro I'd advise you to have whatever motions you wish to submit to this Court at the close of the Commonwealth's case prepared for argument tomorrow. That's all for today. Thank you both."

Both counsel exited chambers to face the delirious mob.

Chapter 27
The Juror at Home

Mary was putting dinner on the table when Bill arrived. His kids were in the living room watching some garbage television. Bill kicked them into the kitchen for dinner and rolled the set to the doorway so he could catch the news during his meal.

Always concerned about Bill's freedom Mary asked: "You gonna watch the news, Bill?"

"Yah, Mary," Bill answered indulging her simplemindedness. "I'm gonna watch the news." Jesus she had become a real bitch during trial, he thought.

Mary could smell the scotch on his breath and held it accountable for his bad mood. "Hows the trial?" she asked gingerly.

Bill had grown impatient with her unrelenting interference. "Jesus, Mary, I ain't supposed to talk about that - am I?" Mary sat silent staring at Bill prompting him to answer.

"It sucks," he said. "All I did was hang around all day for a couple hours of testimony."

"Is it over soon?"

"If I have my way it will." Bill flicked on the television and turned to channel 5. The news was just starting and he commanded silence in the kitchen with a swift slap to his nearest child's head.

The top story was the Domainio trial. Channel 5 flashed a quick sound-bite showing the defense leaving the court house. After the break Bill learned that '. . . sources had told this reporter that the Judge was considering a request made by the defense to strike the testimony of Charlie Bottatelli noted hit man for the mob because he had failed to identify the defendant instead calling him by the name of the deceased victim in the case, Tommy Francone. If so, those same sources informed channel 5 that in all likelihood the Judge would be forced to grant an acquittal of the defendant for lack of evidence in which case Tony Domainio would walk out of the court house a free man.'

Bill dropped his knife and fork in disbelief. "I don't believe it." He said to no one. "I just don't believe it." He looked at Mary. "I don't believe he is going to let him go."

"It's just the news, Billy," Mary said. "They just saying whateva' sounds good. It don't mean nuthin'."

Bill thought about it for a minute. Maybe she was right. The news don't know nothing.

They had been wrong before. Besides, they just said sources told them that. Shit they probably made it up. "Yeah, you're probably right, Mary," he said haltingly. "He wouldn't do that. They'd stone him to death. Nah, he don't got the guts to do that." Bill reached over and clicked off the television. He'd had enough of Tony Dimmainio for one day He was just going to stay in, relax, have a couple of beers, mind to himself, and go to bed early. Tomorrow's a big day. Anticipating having the case in his hands on the morrow, he smiled and dove into his corn beef and cabbage.

Chapter 28
An End?

It was a good day for a funeral. It was a day to respect the present. There was very little meaningless comment; an absence of frivolous conversation. Today was not a day to waste any words. They might never be spoken again. There was a darkness too. As if the world was resigned to a pending trauma and all had dressed for the occasion.

If one had listened to the news that morning the tone of presentation was not as pitched as one might have expected. No fabricated excitement spoken over the fabricated noise of a fabricated crowd. Simply a statement of the inevitable with a question posed. Perhaps an effort to create curiosity rather than to perpetuate sensationalism.

Tony was calm. He sat. He thought. He waited. He knew that today would be the end all of all ends. It was so difficult for him, as it had been and would be for hundreds of thousands of others, to endure not only the uncertainty of a future but the selection of that future by strangers. His life was up for sale and the department of corrections was the highest bidder.

The calculation of years had been completed that morning. He had done what any inmate does awaiting verdict. He had made the various additions and subtractions. Thinking in questions he asked and answered himself: At the least, when would my appeal from conviction and sentencing be heard? 1 1/2 to 2 years. At the least, when would I be eligible for a gubernatorial pardon? Age 78. At the least how long would I live? How many years of jail until death puts me on parole? 30 years from now. At the greatest how old would I be at death?

He could pick and choose that last option. Death might be the only free choice he might have; his last freedom.

Never once did he think of Tommy; his family; his friends.

"Good morning," Judge Wilton had offered as all counsel entered chambers. "Please, have a seat."

"Good morning," all hailed.

When Ron Cleary had appeared Judge Wilton said: "Mr. Cleary, it's good of you to grace us with your presence. This mightn't have anything to do with your own evaluation of the case, would it?" Wilton saw Ron's presence as an open invitation to spar. He readily took the position of the antagonist seeking to set the terms of battle through intimidation.

"I take no position as of yet Judge," Ron had responded evenly. "I am merely here as a spectator/supervisor reviewing the performance of the rank and file."

Judge Wilton received this offer of compromise with skepticism given that Ron had chosen to skirt his challenge and direct his condescension to Carolyn.

"Well, so be it. It is good fortune that you chose to take a seat at this gathering," noting well that on this occasion Ron had commandeered a chair before being ordered to do so. After allowing both Joe and Carolyn the opportunity to restate their respective positions and concerns over Charlie's testimony he spoke more for the court reporter than for those present. "I have reviewed the motions and memoranda submitted and have considered arguments by counsel. Before I go any further I implore counsel to come to terms with an appropriate disposition of this case. If I rule in favor of the Commonwealth, Mr. Balliro, and allow this case to go to the jury I don't think there is any question they will reach a verdict of guilty to some level of homicide. If I decide to rule in favor of the defendant, and throw this case out, you, Miss Cheline, will lose all. Now I know that the Commonwealth has offered second degree in the case. I also know that that has been rejected. Mr. Balliro, is there any reason to believe that the defendant will reconsider the Commonwealth's offer?"

Joe took a moment knowing full well the answer. "In all honesty, your Honor, no,"

"Miss Cheline, or in any event Mr. Cleary, would the Commonwealth be willing to either offer again second degree or in the interests of judicial economy and Las Vegas odds, offer manslaughter with significant time?"

"Neither," Ron answered coolly.

"I see."

Judge Wilton stopped breathing for what seemed an eternity as he selected among the papers strewn upon his desk those of Joe and Carolyn's, submitted on both on the issue of Charlie's testimony and Joe's request for acquittal.

"Carolyn, do you have any other witnesses besides Mr. Bottatelli?"

"I renew my motion on the confidential informant without submission of the Walsh affidavit."

Ron said nothing.

Judge Wilton smiled. "Denied."

"In that case I have no one else your Honor."

"Do you have any reason to believe that Mr. Bottatelli will be able to identify the defendant if he is put on the stand today?"

"Your Honor, Mr. Bottatelli is no longer in the custody of the office of the Suffolk County District Attorney," Carolyn said quietly.

"You do not even have custody?" Wilton said incredulously.

"No, your Honor, the Federal Marshals have served a capias pursuant to a detainer. We have honored it. They have not yet transported him from the court house. He is available to take the stand. I would just need time to contact the D.A."

Naturally suspicious whenever the Federal Government expressed an interest in a state case, Joe could only conclude that there was a Federal indictment out there somewhere that named Charlie and if Charlie were named .....

"Will he be able to continue if you put him on the stand?" Wilton asked again breaking Joe's train of thought.

"Not at this time, no your Honor, I don't believe he could," Carolyn said.

"Understood," Judge Wilton said. "Under these circumstances I have no choice but to allow Mr. Balliro's Motion in Limine. For the record, I have reviewed the transcript of the Voir Dire this Court conducted into the competency of the Commonwealth's witness Charlie Bottatelli. I recognize now that I inadvertently structured a question to the witness to the effect 'Do you realize that you are here for the Anthony Domainio murder trial? That question was fatally defective for it was undoubtedly interpreted by the witness consistent with his belief that the deceased Tommy Francone is alive and was seated at defense table and that he committed the murder of the defendant, Anthony Domainio, upon Mr. Francone's orders. I offer my apologies to the Commonwealth and to the defendant."

"Regardless, this leaves this Court in a precarious situation and the prosecution of the case in a more unenviable position for I find that no legitimate inference can be drawn by this jury that the witness meant the defendant when he spoke of Tommy Francone. I also find that the consequences of allowing this witness to continue under any of these circumstances and with any attempted curative instruction would operate to deny the defendant even the most basic of his rights under the law. The defendant's motion is allowed. Do you intend to rest, Miss Cheline?" he asked.

"Yes, your Honor."

"Very well. Mr. Balliro, is it safe to assume that you will make motion for acquittal once the Commonwealth rests?"

"Yes, your Honor, that is my intention."

"And if denied are you prepared to go forward with your case?"

"I am prepared to go forward your Honor."

"Very well. It is my intention then to bring down the jury so that you, Carolyn, may rest with all due pomp and circumstance. Before you do, however, I will instruct the jury to disregard the testimony of Mr. Bottatelli and to strike it from their memory. Unless, of course, you have objection to that instruction, Mr. Balliro."

"None, your Honor."

I will not hear any argument on the judgment of acquittal. I will rule from the bench. If it is my intention to grant an acquittal it will become readily apparent. If not, I will deny your motion Mr. Balliro and instruct you to proceed. I hope I have left enough suspense to excite your fertile minds."

"Note my objection to the granting of the defendant's motion in limine and to your proposed procedures in front of the jury," Ron said.

"So noted."

"Note my objection to your denial of my motion for judgment of acquittal if you choose to do so your Honor," Joe said.

"So noted."

"If there is nothing else?"

Without waiting for a response Judge Wilton called, "Trevor . . . "

Chapter 29

While those in the court room took their respective seats Judge Wilton stood from his desk in chambers, donned his robe, and prepared to enter the bench.

Ron and Carolyn sat at prosecution's table. They had not spoken after leaving chambers but instead took their respective seats without comment leaving any discussion about the Judge's termination and cancellation of Charlie's testimony unrequited. Carolyn mentally reviewed her notes for the cross examination of Joe's experts.

Joe, Tony, and Julianne sat quiet at defense table. A manila file in front of Joe labeled 'Directed Verdict', containing copies of all the essential motions and memorandum liberally scribbled throughout in Joe's cryptic style, sat somberly as if awaiting the most valuable player award. Unlike Ron and Carolyn, Joe had discussed the ruling on Charlie. He had taken the time to tell Julianne and Tony that should the jury convict they had a legitimate appellate issue because of Charlie's testimony. This, of course, Julianne knew from chambers. The explanation was for Tony's benefit. She shook her head in agreement reinforcing her father's words.

"Do ya think he'll let me go?" Tony had asked.

"I have no way of knowing, Tony," Joe answered. "I'll tell you this; he is going about things in an odd way. Usually he would dismiss the jury and hear the motion for acquittal. He's not going to dismiss the jury after Carolyn does. He is not going to allow any argument beyond the memo," he said with his hand on the folder. "That leads me to believe he is just going to deny the motion and instruct us to call our first witness, who incidentally is the voice analyst."

"Uh huh," was all Tony said.

Judge Wilton entered the court room and took his seat at such a quick stride that there was little time to fully rise before being called to be seated. The normal call to order was preempted by Judge Wilton's almost immediate admonition to those filling the gallery that he would not tolerate outbursts of any kind during his comments and instructions to the jury. Without pause he set to his purpose turning to face the jury while standing.

"Yesterday during the testimony of one Charlie Bottatelli it became necessary for me to call a recess so that I and the attorneys could discuss his testimony. The purpose of that discussion need not concern you. But suffice it to say that the law requires a certain minimum threshold of understanding by any individual before he would be allowed to take the stand and present evidence for your consideration. You will not be hearing from Mr. Bottatelli today or any other day for that matter as concerns this case. I am further instructing you to strike anything you may have heard or may remember about Mr. Bottatelli"s testimony from your memory."

In the jury, Bill Lonnegan leaned forward, mouth open, with a look of disbelief. As the judge continued a small smile curled his lip as he thought: right, you idiot, we will all just erase it like you wipe a blackboard.

Judge Wilton took note of Bill's animation.

"You are not to consider why I have instructed you so. You are not to dwell on anything whatsoever with respect to this person. You will not consider the person or anything about the person during your deliberations. Is that understood?"

All either nodded in affirmation or spoke in acknowledgment.

Judge Wilton turned to Carolyn and Joe without word giving them the customary opportunity to signal a request for side bar to discuss his instruction before he continued.

With no such indication he directed his attention to Carolyn.

"Does the Commonwealth have anything else, Miss Cheline?"

"No, your Honor." She turned to the jury. "That is the Commonwealth's case." She raised her arms, palms up, enjoining the jury, and while turning her head to the bench, she announced: "The Commonwealth rests."

Joe was amused at Carolyn's non-verbal effort to give the jury the impression that she was resting their case not hers. She had appeared awkward and therefore her efforts appeared staged. He made no objection.

"Mr. Balliro?" Judge Wilton asked.

"Yes, your Honor, at this time I would present a motion to the Court."

"Understood, Mr. Balliro."

Wilton looked around the court room lifting the defendant's motion for judgment of acquittal from the bench without sitting. He crossed his hands behind his back and raised his head toward the high ceiling. For a moment he seemed to be contemplating the water stains that darkened the age old molding, his eyes tracing the child-like maze of thread-like cracks.

Joe knew at that moment what Judge Wilton intended to release his client for he would not have sought such drama, he would not have felt the need to express such anguish over the word "Denied".

Carolyn, leaning back in her chair, tossed her pen the short distance from her hands on her lap to a stack of papers on the desk in front of her, a small measure of her disgust at the realization that Wilton was going to do the unforgivable. Ron without movement, a deep glare, the corners of his mouth turned down, wondered just how he could seek retribution upon the judge.

The jury sat in expectation not having the experience to read the nuances of the players' actions. Bill was as much in the dark as any other, even with his "superior" intellect.

Turning to the jury, Judge Wilton sighed. "You have sat patiently and attentively as jurors throughout these past weeks and it has been my honor and pleasure to have had the privilege to sit with you as we go through the steps, always painstakingly, sometimes exhaustively, of our judicial process. It is a time honed system of justice that has developed to its current state of perfection only through such attention to detail. You have had the pleasure of observing two of the finest attorney's in the Commonwealth seek to persuade you of the respective positions. That has been a pleasure for me. I hope it has been likewise for you. As far as my presence - I hope that I have lived up to what you envisioned a judge to be."

Bill was irritated by the judge's ingratiating remarks. Within the last moments he had developed a pending sense of doom.

"As you have seen the Commonwealth has rested. It has finished its case. It is now time for the defense to present evidence, if it wishes, to you. Of course they need do nothing. As I told you before we began, the Commonwealth has the burden. You have respected my wishes," Wilton said while looking directly at Bill. "You have conducted yourselves with integrity and honor and therefore I feel that you deserve this explanation."

More pats on the back. What is this a mutual admiration society? Bill thought.

"Consistent with that burden the Commonwealth must present enough evidence to the Court that would permit a rational juror to find the defendant guilty of the crimes charged. This is known as a threshold showing. Getting over the rail or getting over the bar. The bar being that waist high wall that separates the gallery from you and the attorneys. So you see the Commonwealth must present something more concrete than what the gallery collectively or by majority believes to be true. If not, they cannot go from the gallery, over the bar or rail, and into this protected area where you are seated. This burden is tested by the defendant's motion. The motion just made to the Court. It is a motion asking that I review whether the Commonwealth has come forth with sufficient evidence to warrant a rational trier of fact, you, of finding the defendant guilty. I must rule that they have not."

Despite the court officers' and the judge's remonstrations against outbursts, the commotion in the gallery became uncontrollable.

In the juror's box, Bill Lonnegan moved forward again, now in a numbed and shocked disbelief mouthing: "What the fuck?"

"It is the duty of this Court to grant the motion for a directed verdict and release the defendant," Judge Wilton added quickly, noting Bill's actions. "Thank you Ladies and Gentlemen."

As Judge Wilton turned to leave the bench to avoid the inevitable, and what he knew would be the uncontrollable, increased raucousness of the crowd, Bill stood from his seat and in normal voice said, "Noo." As the realization of Tony slipping his retribution became more of an immediate reality his protestations became louder. "Nooooo!!" he called out to Wilton.

Trevor looked over to see Bill moving around the juror below him with difficulty, attempting to climb over the seat as if he were attempting to exit a crowded movie theater by alternate route. Judge Wilton stopped and turned.

"Sir, sit down," Trevor ordered.

"NOO!" he yelled at Trevor. "NO Fuckin' Way."

Joe, Julianne, and Tony, in the throes of congratulations, and Ron and Carolyn in the process of clearing the desk in disgust, could not help but noticed the clawing movements of Bill with his loud calls of disbelief and dispute.

"What the fuck do you thing you're doing?" he hollered, his hands rose in a questioning gesture as he moved to scale the juror box. "Who The FUCK do YOU THINK YOU ARE?" he yelled at the judge.

"Trevor restrain that man," Wilton ordered.

The court room quieted. The attention of the gallery was now drawn back to the bench.

As Trevor moved towards the jury box, the other jurors cleared away from the seats Bill was attempting to climb. The foot on his bad leg caught on the back of the seat in front of him and he fell awkwardly forward still clamoring and reaching out in front of him as he tumbled. "That FUCKIN' Guy is FUCKIN' Guilty you stupid FUCK!!!! DON'T LET HIM GO YOU CHICKENSHIT. HE'S FUCKIN' GUILTY. Bill could be heard yelling from somewhere between the chairs physically out of view of all but the jurors.

Trevor had circled the small area between the witness box and the end of the juror box where Bill seemed to have fallen. The other court officers were behind him. Suddenly and without warning Bill was up between the two levels of the juror box midway between both ends, over the waist high rail and heading for Tony.

"Stop him, Trevor!!" Judge Wilton yelled, but it was too late. Bill knocked Joe away and grabbed Tony around the neck knocking Julianne into her seat.

Tony reacted with street instinct. He raised his arms above Bill's, swung his body first to the right then to the left striking Bill in the jaw four times with his fists and elbows in the matter of microseconds. Stepping back once and then quickly forward, he struck upward against Bill's elbows with his palms forcing Bill to release a tenacious grip around his throat. Once free of Bill's hold, Tony struck upward again with the base of his palm contacting the bridge of Bill's nose crushing bone and releasing a torrent of blood. As Bill began to melt to the floor Tony moved sideways lifted his foot and stomped down viciously on the side of Bill's bad knee snapping his leg like a twig, once again. In a matter of seconds Bill lay unconscious on the floor. Tony looked down at Bill. "I'll be damned. It's fuckin' Lonnegan," he said with a smile. "What a stupid fuck."

During this brief foray, two men from the gallery had moved quickly from their position at the back wall, pushing the crowd apart as they strove to near the bar area. As the first man neared where Gaetano was seated, he reached into his jacket. Gaetano stuck his foot out surreptitiously from the pew. The first Federal Marshal tripped and fell. As he struck the floor at the foot of the bar rail, his hand jostled the trigger of his .38, then partly nestled in his shoulder holster. It fired taking out a large chunk of flesh in the Marshal's arm, the projectile passing through and lodging in the wall behind the court officer's desk with a rain of splinters.

Immediately the gallery, the attorney's and the Judge dove for the floor.

Tony had reached for two heavy law books that had sat innocently on defense counsel's desk every day over the past week and had raised them over his head in ready position to strike the back of Bill's exposed neck when the firearm discharged, freezing his motion. Microseconds later, two other .38's in the hands of Larry and Trevor pointed purposely at his head.

The second Federal Marshal stepped over his injured partner, squatted in combat stance, gun drawn; elbows resting on the bar rail, and directed the muzzle of his police issue at Tony's head.

The first marshal could be heard to groan loudly with intermittent curse.

After a moment of the type of anxious silence likened to that of the eye of the storm, Judge Wilton, now abjectly furious, hollered, "ENOUGH, ENOUGH!!", as he pounded a book on the top of the bench. Directing his attention to the Marshal with arms mounted offensively he said, "WHAT IS THE MEANING OF THIS INTRUSION SIR!!!

YOU DARE TO BRING WEAPONS INTO MY COURT ROOM!!! Without waiting for a response he turned to Trevor and said, "TREVOR, LOWER YOUR WEAPONS AND RELEASE MR. DOMAINIO. CALL THE MEDICS, AND GET THIS JURY OUT OF HERE!"

Trevor signaled Larry, who had lowered his gun as the moment had passed, to call down for medical assistance. Trevor lowered his gun but did not release Tony. The Marshal reholstered his weapon. The gallery rose.

Joe was now standing next to Trevor, Julianne watching the labored breathing of the prone Bill.

Carolyn and Ron were standing cautiously.

"Your Honor, before I release Mr. Domainio there are two gentlemen, well now one, who would ask to speak to you," Trevor said.

"Your Honor, I am special agent Thomas Shriver of the United States Attorney's Office," directing the Judge's attention to the marshal now leaning against the wall, his hand stanching the flow of blood as he waited for assistance, Shriver continued, "This is Federal Marshal Peter Costa. We have a warrant for the arrest of Antonio Domainio on charges of violations of the Racketeering and Influenced

Corrupt Organizations Act. A 157 page indictment was handed down three weeks ago by a secret grand jury of the United States District Court. Mr. Domainio is named as a principal. I would ask that you order custody transferred. We already have Mr. Calhoun and have held him awaiting your ruling."

Tony looked at Joe without expression. Trevor handed the warrant to the clerk who then passed it to the Judge.

"Everything is in order," Judge Wilton said after reviewing the papers. "Trevor, you are to ensure that all transfer documents are in order and are to transfer custody of the defendant Antonio Domainio to the custody of the Federal Marshals. Understood?"

"Yes, your Honor."

"Get him out of my court room," Judge Wilton ordered with disdain. "And Trevor?" Trevor looked up. "Clean this place up and throw out the trash," he ordered pointing at Bill. Judge Wilton lifted up his robe with one hand and drew down the zipper with the other as he walked without fanfare into chambers.

Larry escorted the remaining jurors past the unconscious body of Bill, through the side door, releasing them to find their own way upstairs to the juror room and the elevator to the lobby.

Joe turned to Tony. "The defense of Tony Domainio - the sequel - part two."

Tony looked at Joe with an appreciative smile. "Yah, Joe. See yah."

Tony was escorted back to his privileged single cell of concrete block and iron bars.

As the court room cleared with most of the crowd converging on Joe and Carolyn in the hallway outside, it was obvious that one man remained seated as he had throughout the events of that morning. Gaetano, in disguise, sat still, controlling his anger, channeling his stress, taking his doctor's advice. He sat still for quite a while, his body calmed by a darkened serenity. Time was not a concern. He had, after all, much to face; a lot of work to do, many people to see. He would not make them happy. It was now his job not to make them happy.

But before he began, here, of all places, he would rest.

Epilogue

The federal government was a formidable competitor. The battles waged in the state courts paled in comparison to the war that could be fought in the United States District Court for the District of Massachusetts. The rules were radically different there, much more designed to insure conviction, far less protective of the accused.

Joe had explained these things in short form to Tony after he had been returned to his cell awaiting transfer. The first step would be the pre-trial detention hearing that would occur in the upcoming week in front of a magistrate at the Federal Court House at Post Office Square. Unlike a simple bail hearing the pre-trial detention hearing required substantial preparation and presentation, the burden on the defendant, the court more inclined to detain prior to trial. Joe would see Tony again, in a matter of days, to begin again. For now he accepted congratulations from Tony and well wishes for a relaxing weekend. He stood to leave. "How about that Lonnegan, Joe," Tony said. "Think I can get his brother on my Fed trial?"

"I doubt it Tony. One thing's for certain, you won't get him."

"Right, Joe. One thing is for certain, I'll make sure he's nice and comfortable in here." Tony smiled that wicked smile.

Back at Harbor Towers, Joe felt eased at the absence of media. Reaching over, he lifted the receiver off the cradle to make certain he would not be bothered. Of all the times of rest and peace it seemed that the evening of the final day of a trial, whatever its outcome is the most appealing. With an unnecessary fire snapping, a small lamp perched over his shoulder, and a glass of Beaujolais on the small table to his left, Joe steeped himself happily in this much anticipated detachment.

Allowing his head to fall back, he dozed solidly for a few minutes waking himself with a jolt. Time to go to bed, he thought, enough of this.

He was exhausted and in that exhausted state he realized that he did not want to manipulate, he did not want to make choices that affected other people's lives, he did not want to carry those absolutes of his profession into his private world. Joe stood and moved toward his bedroom. He laughed a little at himself. He knew he would wake in a couple of hours, unable to stop his mind from racing threw the next trial he had on the agenda. This one was bad, Kiddy-diddler. Very creepy client.

Hell, maybe sometimes it was just a grind - no fun. Nah, he thought, it's all fun.

Joe turned his back and walked out of his study, a gratifying yawn accompanying his stride.

THE END

Made in United States
North Haven, CT
12 August 2022

22625546R00205